BISTROT BRUNO

COOKING FROM

BISTROT BRUNO

COOKING FROM

BRUNO LOUBET

TEXT IN ASSOCIATION WITH
NORMA MACMILLAN
PHOTOGRAPHS BY
JASON LOWE

MACMILLAN

First published 1995 by Macmillan Reference Books

a division of Macmillan Publishers Limited
25 Eccleston Place, London SW1W 9NF
and Basingstoke

Associated companies throughout the world

ISBN 0 333 61140 3

9 8 7 6 5 4 3 2 1

A CIP catalogue record for this book is available from
the British Library

Designed by Peter Ward
Typeset by Parker Typesetting Service, Leicester
Printed and bound in Great Britain by The Bath Press, Avon

FOR ALL FOOD LOVERS

CONTENTS

I would like to thank my publishers, Macmillan, for their understanding and support whilst writing this book, and Norma MacMillan, my co-author, for her invaluable patience.

LIST OF PLATES

An Important Note about Measurements and Ingredients

In the recipes, two and sometimes three sets of measurements are given for ingredients. These are metric weights and measures, followed by their nearest equivalent in pounds and ounces, and then, when required, a third measurement in American cups and spoons. When preparing a recipe, follow only one set of measurements because they are not exact equivalents and cannot be used interchangeably with any success.

Where ingredient names and terms in the method differ for the US, the American equivalent is given in parentheses.

Where a recipe calls for sugar, this is granulated sugar. Other types of sugar are specified. Please note that British granulated sugar is coarser than American granulated sugar, and in some cases British cooks are advised to use the finer caster sugar where American cooks can use their granulated.

FOREWORD

I met Bruno Loubet at a party in London in 1992. A quiet, seemingly shy man, he was sitting placidly on the sofa and cradling a bowl of curry. We talked for an hour – mostly about parsnips – and at the end of the evening he suggested I visit the Four Seasons Restaurant, where he was then Head Chef, to cook for a day. It was thrilling and after coming back for another day, I accepted an offer to work there for six months.

When Bruno enters a kitchen he undergoes a startling transformation, catalysed by the proximity of food. He waltzes through his work with the passion and dexterity of a dancer, his talent for invention and undiminished enthusiasm for cooking inspiring staggering loyalty in his brigade. He is proud of his work – he knows that he has a special gift – but this pride never spills over into arrogance. Where some other chefs rule their underlings in conditions of brutal – even vicious – tyranny, his natural ability and charm drive others with the aspiration to imitate his achievements.

It is not hard to pin down the strength of Bruno's cooking. Like many chefs he has a deep respect for traditional recipes – if it works don't fix it – but he complements this with a bold innovative streak to combat the fatigue bred of familiarity. Where he differs from the others is that these new combinations, however bizarre they look on paper, once tasted seem to belong together as surely as basil and tomato, orange and cardamom, or carrot and ginger.

This is not quirkiness for its own sake: once you have eaten the rabbit with lime pickle potatoes or the divine scallops and black pudding on mash with parsley and garlic sauce, you cannot help feeling that these things were always meant to be together. It was just a matter of time until someone made the marriage. Many chefs would be delighted to make one such match during their careers. It is a mark of his exceptional talent that Bruno has already made several. Here is your chance to try some of them.

HENRY DIMBLEBY

INTRODUCTION

Is it bistro or bistrot? Well, to me, both spellings are correct. But what kind of food should be served in a bistrot? I am tempted to say only good food, but that wouldn't really be an answer. Let me try to set out my ideas about what a bistrot is today.

Gone are the days when a bistrot meal would start with two or three pâtés and a jar of pickles, followed by a beef stew accompanied by mashed potatoes, a cheese selection that included a perfectly ripe Camembert or goat's cheese, and then the *coup de grâce* – an apple tart topped with vanilla ice cream. In truth, I don't know many people who could do this meal justice: our modern lifestyle precludes such consumption. Also, this would not be commercially viable today.

I think that bistrots in the Nineties should almost be synonymous with fast food places, the major difference being that in a bistrot better food is served personally in more comfortable surroundings. Thus, value-wise you are better off in a bistrot.

To my mind, 'value for money' are the key words in bistrot cooking. This means using cheaper cuts of meat, the less fashionable vegetables and an unfussy approach. These give the bistrot a great advantage: it can offer fair prices and still make a profit, thus allowing the business to prosper.

There is really no excuse for a bistrot chef not to have a creative menu as today the choice of raw ingredients is so vast. I am always looking for new foods to add to the already wide range used in my kitchen. For example, I now make my own curry mix (see page 210) and do not hesitate to use preserved black beans, chilli or ginger when preparing an old-fashioned dish such as tripe (see page 127). Good cooking starts with good quality and diverse ingredients.

When I started cooking in England, in 1982, my knowledge was not so great, but my views on cooking were already formed. Nouvelle cuisine, which was then reaching its zenith, did little for me. No, I was still anchored firmly to the daubes, pâtés, confit, soups and tarts of my French heritage. Over the years I have made changes and added to my repertoire, sometimes tweaking old classics and sometimes creating my own dishes. I try hard not to be obsessive with fussy techniques because I think this detracts from the original idea, the natural flavours and appearance.

I have often been asked where I find the inspiration for new dishes. I can only reply that I agree with the famous French sculptor, Armand, who once said that 'the base of creativity is more intuition than imagination'. This was obviously the view held by Alain Chapel too, who said 'cooking is not only in recipes'. I think that you must taste and taste again, perhaps adding more herbs, a dash of vinegar for acidity or simply a pinch of salt. Tasting is what it is all about.

A recipe may suggest a garnish of spinach, but why not try broccoli purée? This is where the cook will learn and begin to think for himself, to marry flavours, to let the taste imagination work, to be a little daring, letting intuition guide and gaining experience. This is how I work. If you use your own senses and enjoy the processes of cooking, that love and dedication will permeate the food and thrill your guests. Even when shopping, use your feelings; go with no preconceived ideas, but let your eyes, nose and imagination – and, of course, your purse – direct your instincts. Be bold and try new ingredients.

Whilst in France recently, I ate in many bistrots and restaurants with no pretensions to stardom. Some were good and others not so good – yes, even in France we have our failures! It was clear that a new generation of restaurateurs had emerged, with new ideas, new concepts, and chefs who are not resting on the laurels of French cuisine. These chefs are not afraid to break the rules and challenge the inherited precepts, good or bad, of the *ancien régime*. Top quality ingredients and simplicity are the bywords of this new generation.

At the forefront of this movement is Pierre Gagnaire, for whom I have the greatest admiration. He was the precursor of this new generation of chefs and even today, with his incomparable 'avant garde' style, he rises to new heights in his wonderful restaurant in the heart of St Etienne. The guides, Michelin included, have awarded him top honours (3 stars, normally reserved for the far more classic school), which bodes well for the new generation of chefs who will be encouraged by Pierre Gagnaire's success. He has also opened up a bistrot in St Etienne where his culinary ambitions and flights of fancy can be enjoyed by a wider clientele.

In addition to recipes from Pierre Gagnaire's bistrot, I have included some from other restaurants in France, some not so famous but all stars in their own right. These illustrate the different styles of the new chefs, and are my way of honouring their achievements.

Some Useful Ingredients

The following is a list of ingredients that I think are most useful to have on hand in the kitchen:

mild lime pickle

tandoori paste

Dijon mustard

dark soy sauce

Worcestershire sauce

HP sauce

tomato ketchup

mango chutney

creamed horseradish

pesto

tomato paste (in a tube)

red wine vinegar

tarragon vinegar

balsamic vinegar

vegetable oil

extra virgin olive oil (for seasoning)

virgin olive oil (for cooking)

black olives

green peppercorns in brine (these
    keep a long time in the
    refrigerator)

gherkins

Maggi chicken stock cubes

a piece of Parmesan (in the
    refrigerator)

fine table salt

Maldon sea salt

grey rock salt

black peppercorns in a mill

turmeric

mustard seeds

dried provençal herbs

ground allspice

cloves

cardamom pods

fennel seeds

coriander seeds

juniper berries

celery salt

saffron threads

garlic

dried thyme

dried bay leaves

dried orange peel

caster (granulated) sugar

icing (confectioners') sugar

plain (all-purpose) flour

self-raising flour

baking powder

vanilla pods (beans)

short-grain pudding rice

basmati rice

dried tagliatelle

orange flower water

Some Tips in the Kitchen

Peeling and crushing or chopping garlic is always a smelly and messy job, so prepare it in large quantities – 3 heads at time. Mix the crushed or chopped garlic cloves with a bit of olive oil and a pinch of salt in a jar, and cover with a film of oil. Close the jar tightly with cling film and a lid. When you use some of the garlic, smooth the film of oil again. The garlic will keep in the refrigerator for up to 2 weeks.

Use a potato peeler to take shavings from a piece of Parmesan.

If you are adding parsley to a sauce, blanch it first in boiling water for 5 seconds and then refresh. The parsley flavour will permeate the sauce more fully.

Use a coffee grinder or spice mill for grinding spices.

Always buy spices in small quantities.

If radishes or spring onions (scallions) feel a bit limp and soft, leave them in iced water for 5 minutes. They will then be crisp again.

To keep asparagus fresh in the refrigerator, wrap the spears in a wet cloth and stand them tips up.

When you cook asparagus in boiling water, tie the spears together in a bunch with string so that the tips will not be damaged.

When preparing a sauce using bones, particularly game bones and trimmings, add a few ice cubes from time to time during the reduction period. This will cause all the impurities and fat to rise to the surface so they can be skimmed off easily.

To prevent fruit from falling to the bottom of a fruit cake, first toss the fruit in a little flour to give it a very light coating.

Before roasting a duck that seems very fatty, make several incisions in the skin with a sharp knife, immerse the duck in boiling water and simmer for 3 minutes. Some of the fat will melt away. Drain and dry the duck, and it is ready for roasting.

If your red wine sauce is too acid, add a teaspoon of blackcurrant or redcurrant jelly.

To make a lemon more juicy, roll it on the work surface with the palm of your hand before cutting it and squeezing out the juice.

To keep your chopping board stationary, lay a few wet paper towels on the work surface and set the board on top.

If you are making mayonnaise and it starts to split, don't worry. Put a spoonful of hot water in a small bowl, add a spoonful of the split mayonnaise and mix well, then very slowly add the rest of the mayonnaise, whisking constantly. This rescue method will also work for béarnaise sauce.

When cleaning mushrooms don't leave them in water because they will soak it up like a sponge. Dip them one by one in water and brush away any dirt or soil with a small brush.

Always add some water to your salad dressings. They will be lighter and the water will help with the emulsion.

It's quite convenient to melt chocolate in the microwave, but watch carefully to be sure you don't scorch it.

When I am cooking at home, in what my wife likes to call *her* kitchen, if I don't have any home-made stock I often use 2 Maggi chicken stock cubes dissolved in 500 ml/16 fl oz hot water. If I need a dark stock, I add a few drops of dark soy sauce. You can also flavour the stock by simmering it with a clove of garlic and a few celery leaves for 5 minutes. Take care when adding salt as you may not need any at all.

When you have roasted a chicken, keep the carcass. Also keep any bones from beef and veal. Freeze all of these. When you have enough bones, put them together with a *mirepoix* to make a meat bouillon. This will be a wonderful stock for a risotto or a tasty soup.

Before peeling button onions or shallots, soak them in cold water for 10 minutes. This will make the peeling much easier.

When using a vanilla pod (bean) in a cream, split the pod lengthways in half and scrape the seeds into the cream.

FIRST COURSES

In bistrots, a first course is rarely complicated.
A good fragrant soup, a moist coarse pâté, a simple
leek salad are all appropriate. Here I have tried to go
a step further, to add a personal touch to a dish
when possible, but still keeping in mind simplicity
and taste.

Soups

Veal Bouillon with Angel Hair and Chervil

Bouillon de Veau aux Cheveux d'Ange et Cerfeuil

8 servings

1.5 kg/3¼ lb meaty flat veal ribs (breast riblets)

3 litres/4⅔ pints/3 quarts water

200 g/7 oz carrots

200 g/7 oz leeks

100 g/3½ oz celery

200 g/7 oz onions

150 g/5 oz turnips

4 garlic cloves, crushed with the side of a knife

500 ml/16 fl oz white wine

a few sprigs of fresh flat-leaf parsley

½ fresh or 1 small dried bay leaf

1 clove

1 tsp celery salt

6 black peppercorns, coarsely crushed

85 g/3 oz angel hair pasta

4 tbsp chopped fresh chervil

Put the veal ribs in a large pot and pour over the water. Bring to the boil, skimming occasionally. Leave to simmer gently for 30 minutes.

Add 10 ice cubes. Bring back to the boil and skim again. Cut all the vegetables into 3–4 cm/1¼–1½ inch chunks. Add to the pot together with the garlic, wine, herbs, clove, celery salt and peppercorns. Leave to simmer for 4 hours.

Strain the bouillon through a colander set in a large bowl, then pour it through a fine sieve into a clean pan. Bring to the boil. Add the angel hair pasta, then remove the pan from the heat and cover. Leave for 2 minutes. Stir in the chervil and serve.

- The ice cubes will encourage fat and impurities to rise to the surface so they can be skimmed off.

- Do not skim the fat completely because a little will add richness to the bouillon.

- Keep the meat and vegetables after straining the bouillon. They can be diced and served cold, dressed with vinaigrette and mixed with chopped onions and French (thin green) beans.

Gratinated Onion and Cider Soup

Soupe à l'Oignon

Did you know that onions crossed the Channel to England from France with William the Conqueror's invaders in 1066? Armies then always had supplies of onions because they are easy to store and keep for a long time. I'm not sure when onion soup crossed the Channel – maybe Paul Bocuse's fame had something to do with it! In any case, onions, like garlic, are still very French, and onion soup is to French bistrots what frites are to steak: simply inseparable. Here I give you my version.

---

30 g/1 oz/2 tbsp butter

400 g/14 oz onions, thinly sliced

2 garlic cloves, chopped

1 bunch of fresh thyme

200 ml/7 fl oz dry (dry hard) cider

2 tbsp soy sauce

1 litre/1$\frac{2}{3}$ pints/1 quart beef bouillon (see note)

salt and freshly ground pepper

8 slices of baguette, toasted

120 g/4 oz Gruyère cheese, grated

4 servings

In a heavy-based saucepan (Le Creuset type), melt the butter. Add the onions and cook gently until they are softened and lightly coloured, stirring from time to time. Add the garlic, thyme and cider and bring to the boil. Boil until reduced by half.

Add the beef bouillon and soy sauce. Bring back to the boil, then reduce the heat and leave to simmer for 1 hour.

Preheat the grill (broiler).

Taste the soup and add salt and pepper. Pour the soup into flameproof bowls, or a large flameproof dish. Add the slices of baguette and sprinkle the cheese over the top. Place under the grill to melt and lightly brown the cheese, then serve very hot.

Bruno's note

● For this soup you need a good, well-flavoured bouillon. To make this, use the same ingredients you would use for a beef stock, but do not roast the bones and vegetables to brown and caramelize them. Just cover beef bones, flavouring vegetables and herbs with water and simmer gently for quite a long time, skimming well to remove all impurities that rise to the surface. After straining, you can add a little colour to the bouillon with a few drops of soy sauce. Alternatively, you can use canned beef consommé or the fresh beef stock now sold in many supermarkets.

Broad Bean and Lovage Soup

Soupe de Fèves à la Lièche

---

4 servings

100 g/3½ oz leeks, chopped
60 g/2 oz/4 tbsp butter
1 garlic clove, chopped
500 ml/16 fl oz strong chicken
    stock
salt and freshly ground pepper

300 g/10 oz shelled fresh broad
    (fava) beans
100 ml/3½ fl oz double (heavy)
    cream
1 tsp chopped fresh lovage
¼ lemon

Cook the leeks in half the butter in a saucepan until soft. Add the garlic and stock and bring to simmering point. Season with salt and pepper.

Add the broad beans and leave to simmer for about 10 minutes. Add the cream and the remaining butter. Pour into a blender and blend until smooth. Press through a fine sieve into a clean pan. Reheat briefly. Add the lovage and a squeeze of lemon. Check the seasoning, and serve.

- Celery leaves or fresh coriander (cilantro) can be substituted for lovage.

- If using older broad beans, which may have tough skins, the skins should be removed. To do this, blanch the beans for 30 seconds, drain and refresh, then squeeze each bean gently to slip off the skin. There is no need to skin young and tender beans.

Leek and Potato Soup with a Dash of Olive Oil

Potage Parmentier à l'Huile d'Olive

This soup is the simplest, most basic preparation you can imagine, but it is delicious. My mother used to make this soup for supper on Sunday evenings, when we had had a large lunch.

Sometimes she would add shredded sorrel leaves, or whisk in an egg just before serving to make threads of yellow and white. I think extra virgin olive oil is a good finishing touch.

4 servings

350 g/12 oz potatoes, preferably King Edwards

2 tbsp olive oil

500 g/1 lb 2 oz leeks, chopped

1 garlic clove, chopped

salt and freshly ground black pepper

1.2 litres/2 pints/5 cups water

extra virgin olive oil, to finish

Peel the potatoes and cut into 2 cm/$\frac{3}{4}$ inch cubes.

Heat the olive oil in a large saucepan. Add the leeks and garlic and cook gently until the leeks start to soften. Stir occasionally. Add the potatoes and season with salt and pepper. Pour in the water. Bring to the boil, then cover and leave to simmer for 45 minutes.

Ladle the soup into bowls or soup plates. Add a splash of extra virgin olive oil to each and a grinding of black pepper and serve.

Affordable Fish Soup

Soupe de Poisson Bon Marché

At the Bistrot, when I have a lot of fish bones – from sole, red mullet, john dory and so on – I always make a fish soup. I love fish soup. On my days off, if I fancy making fish soup I have to go to the fishmonger and spend a fortune on fish. So I realize that a classic recipe for the home cook is out of the question for most people. That's why I devised the one here, for a fish soup that is full of flavour but not so expensive.

4 servings

150 g/5 oz leeks

100 g/3½ oz carrots

100 g/3½ oz celery

3½ tbsp olive oil

3 garlic cloves, crushed with the
side of a knife

½ tbsp dried *herbes de Provence*

1 star anise, coarsely crushed with
the base of a heavy pan

4 cardamom pods, coarsely crushed

1 strip of orange zest

1 tsp green masala curry paste

1 mackerel, weighing 350 g/12 oz,
cleaned and cut across into thick
slices

1 plaice or flounder, weighing
350 g/12 oz, cleaned and cut
across into thick slices

1 tbsp tomato paste

1.5 litres/2⅔ pints/1½ quarts cold
water

1 kg/2¼ lb fresh mussels, well
scrubbed

150 ml/5 fl oz white wine

12 saffron strands soaked in 1 tbsp
water

salt and freshly ground black
pepper

TO SERVE

garlic croûtons (see below)

grated Gruyère cheese

rouille (page 202)

Finely chop the leeks, carrots and celery. Heat the olive oil in a large pot. Add all the chopped vegetables, the garlic, herbs, star anise, cardamom pods, orange zest and masala curry paste. Cook until the vegetables soften, stirring occasionally. This will take at least 5 minutes. Add the mackerel and plaice and stir in the tomato paste. Cook for 3 minutes, then pour in the cold

MUSSELS COOKED ON A PINE BOARD WITH PINE NEEDLES, *PAGE 29*

WARM LEEK SALAD WITH POACHED EGGS AND LARDONS, *PAGE 38*

water. Bring to the boil, skimming off any foam that rises to the surface. Cover and leave to simmer for 45 minutes.

Meanwhile, put the mussels in a pan with the white wine. Cover the pan and put over a high heat. Steam the mussels until the shells open, shaking the pan from time to time. Drain the mussels in a colander set in a large bowl. Set the mussels aside, and add the cooking liquid to the fish soup.

With a hand blender, blend the soup to a smooth texture (or do this in a food processor), then pass it through a fine sieve set in a bowl, pressing out as much of the liquid as possible. Repeat the sieving, then pour the soup into a clean saucepan. Bring to the boil. Add the saffron and check the seasoning. Simmer for 5 minutes.

Add the mussels to the soup. Serve with garlic croûtons, grated Gruyère and rouille.

- Discard any mussels that remain closed when the rest have opened because these will be dead or full of sand.   **Bruno's notes**
- If you prefer, put the *herbes de Provence*, star anise and cardamom pods in a spice mill or coffee grinder and whiz to a coarse powder.
- Just before serving, you could add a dash of Pernod.
- To make garlic croûtons, drizzle thin slices of baguette with olive oil, spread them out on a baking sheet and toast in a moderate oven until crisp and golden brown. Then rub them with a halved garlic clove.
- You can also spread the croûtons with a bit of pesto.

Salmon Velouté Flavoured with Green Peppercorns and Dill

Velouté de Saumon au Poivre Vert et Aneth

These days, salmon is no longer an expensive fish, due mainly to salmon farming in Scotland. The quality of Scottish salmon is guaranteed by a tartan marque, which is comparable to the French *label rouge* – a symbol of maintained high quality. The Scots can feel proud to have this mark of distinction, the only product to have been so honoured outside France.

---

4 servings

1 salmon head

85 g/3 oz /6 tbsp butter

200 g/7 oz leeks, finely chopped

100 g/$3\frac{1}{2}$ oz celery, finely chopped

a few parsley stalks

200 ml/7 fl oz Noilly Prat

1 litre/$1\frac{2}{3}$ pints/1 quart water

40 g/$1\frac{1}{4}$ oz/5 tbsp flour

salt and freshly ground pepper

100 ml/$3\frac{1}{2}$ fl oz double (heavy) cream

12 green peppercorns packed in brine

$\frac{1}{2}$ lemon

1 tsp chopped fresh dill

Cut the salmon head in half and pull out the gills (or ask your fishmonger to do this). Immerse the head in cold water and leave to soak for 30 minutes.

Melt half of the butter in a large saucepan. Add the leeks, celery and parsley stalks and cook gently until soft but not coloured. Add the Noilly Prat and the drained salmon head and stir to mix with the vegetables. Bring the wine to the boil and boil to reduce to about half. Pour in the water. Bring back to the boil and leave to simmer for about 20 minutes. Strain the stock through a fine sieve set in a large bowl.

Melt the remaining butter in a clean saucepan. Heat until it is foamy, then stir in the flour. Cook, stirring, for about 1 minute or until the mixture starts to bubble and turn white. Slowly add the salmon stock, mixing well. Season with salt and pepper, then leave to simmer for 30 minutes.

Add the cream and green peppercorns. Cook for a further 5 minutes.

Just before serving, add a squeeze of lemon juice and the dill.

Root Vegetable and Haggis Soup

Soupe de Légumes d'Hiver et Haggis

The smell of a good soup is reassuring and always welcome. My father wouldn't dream of having a meal without soup as a starter, so the appetizing aromas of a veal bouillon or a vegetable or onion soup would always permeate our house. I often ask myself why the simple vegetable soup my mother used to make always smelled and tasted so good. Even if I use the same ingredients, the result seems to be different. Maybe the organically grown vegetables from the family garden were the secret. The recipe here is based on my mother's, with haggis added to give more depth of flavour.

		6 servings
250 g/9 oz carrots	1 sprig of fresh thyme	
150 g/5 oz parsnips	$\frac{1}{2}$ dried bay leaf	
200 g/7 oz turnips	coarse sea salt	
150 g/5 oz swede (rutabaga)	1 haggis, weighing about 500 g/	
200 g/7 oz leeks	1 lb 2 oz	
100 g/3$\frac{1}{2}$ oz celeriac (celery root)	salt and freshly ground black	
2 garlic cloves, crushed with the	pepper	
side of a knife		

Cut all the vegetables into bite-size chunks. Put them in a large pot with the garlic, thyme and bay leaf. Add enough water to come 5 cm/2 inches above the vegetables and season with sea salt. Peel the haggis and cut it into 4 pieces. Add to the pot.

Bring to the boil, then cover and leave to simmer for 1$\frac{1}{2}$ hours.

Skim any fat from the surface. Taste the soup and add salt and pepper. Serve very hot.

Bouillon Santé

This is the ideal cure for anybody who is feeling miserable and unwell after a great feast, having had too much to eat and drink!

2 servings

400 ml/14 fl oz water

4 garlic cloves, chopped

salt

5 fresh sage leaves

1 sprig of fresh thyme

1 bay leaf

2 tbsp olive oil

Put the water in a saucepan with the garlic and a good pinch of salt. Bring to the boil and simmer for 10 minutes. Add the remaining ingredients, cover and remove from the heat. Leave to cool.

Strain through a fine sieve into a clean pan and bring back to the boil. Serve very hot.

Appetizers

Smoked Mackerel Rillettes on Tomato Salad

Rillettes de Maquereaux Fumé sur Salade de Tomate

This dish is a typical example of my philosophy of cooking: simple ingredients with a simple preparation can give a result that is as good as when using something more expensive and sophisticated.

---

2 smoked mackerel fillets, skinned

85 g/3 oz/6 tbsp soft butter

6 tbsp plain yogurt

$\frac{1}{2}$ lemon

3 pinches of paprika

salt

500 g/1 lb 2 oz ripe plum-type
   tomatoes

4 tbsp lemon dressing (page 205)

120 g/4 oz spring onions (scallions)
   or red onions, chopped

toasted slices of baguette, to serve

4 servings

Put the mackerel in a food processor with the butter, yogurt, lemon juice and paprika. Season with salt. Blend for about 30 seconds or until smooth.

Spoon the rillettes into a bowl, cover and chill.

Slice the tomatoes and arrange on the plates, slightly overlapping like the top of an apple tart. Sprinkle with the dressing and the spring onions.

Using 2 tablespoons dipped in warm water, shape the rillettes into 4 oval- or egg-shaped *quenelles*. Set one carefully in the centre of each plate. Serve with toasted baguette.

Gratinated Oysters with Black Beans and Garlic

Huîtres Gratinées à l'Ail et Haricot Noir Fermenté

I can remember when I first discovered black bean and garlic sauce. It was very exciting – a flavour I hadn't encountered before. I tried it in lots of different dishes for a couple of weeks and then moved on to something else. A few years later I was eating an oyster and it suddenly occurred to me that black bean and garlic sauce would match the strong flavour of fresh oysters without overpowering it. As you develop your palate, tasting many different flavours, your memory stores the information for later reference, so it's a good idea to be adventurous and to try new and unfamiliar foods whenever you can.

4 servings

24 fresh oysters

4 tbsp bottled Chinese black bean and garlic sauce

8 spring onions (scallions), finely chopped

$\frac{1}{2}$ lemon

100 ml/$3\frac{1}{2}$ fl oz olive oil

freshly ground pepper

100 g/$3\frac{1}{2}$ oz/2 cups fine brioche crumbs

Preheat the grill (broiler) to high.

Open the oysters, leaving them on the bottom shells. Pour off the liquor from the shells and arrange the oysters on a baking tray.

Spoon a bit of black bean and garlic sauce on each oyster. Sprinkle with spring onions and add a squeeze of lemon and a dash of olive oil. Season with pepper. Sprinkle the crumbs on top.

Just before serving, place the oysters under the very hot grill and gratinate for 1 minute. It's ready!

My father used to eat up to 5 dozen oysters with a few *crépinettes* for his lunch. Oysters are very nutritious and people say that they are also an aphrodisiac. Is this the reason I have 4 sisters and 2 brothers?

Oysters and Crépinettes

Huîtres et Crépinettes

1 tbsp finely chopped shallot	2 garlic cloves, chopped	**4 servings**
100 ml/$3\frac{1}{2}$ fl oz white wine vinegar	1 tsp brandy	
16 fresh oysters	$\frac{1}{4}$ tsp five spice powder	
	1 tsp Dijon mustard	
FOR THE CRÉPINETTES	a drop of Tabasco sauce	
300 g/10 oz boneless pork neck or	salt and freshly ground pepper	
shoulder	60 g/2 oz pork caul	
100 g/$3\frac{1}{2}$ oz pork back fat	vegetable oil	

Mince (grind) the pork and fat. Place in a bowl and add the garlic, brandy, five spice, mustard and Tabasco. Season with salt and pepper. Cover and leave in a cool place for 24 hours.

Shape the pork mixture into 4 balls and wrap in the caul.

Mix the shallot with the vinegar. Set aside.

Open the oysters and empty out the liquor from the shells. They will make a new batch of liquor in a few minutes and this will be much better.

Heat a film of oil in a frying pan and colour the *crépinettes* on both sides. Reduce the heat and finish the cooking like a sausage.

Set a *crépinette* in the centre of each plate and arrange the oysters around it. Serve the shallot vinegar in a sauceboat.

Oyster Fritters, 'Gribiche' Sauce

Beignets d'Huîtres, Sauce Gribiche

Since I was a child, oysters have been a part of my diet. Where I come from, oysters can be found in every fishmonger and supermarket, and even on display along the road. Oysters from Olèron and Arcachon are widely available everywhere in the area at a reasonable price.

A few years ago I discovered a beautiful Irish oyster from Galway Bay, thanks to Wayne, who is now my regular supplier and also my friend. Sometimes when you remember a flavour from your childhood, nothing will better it, but I must admit that these oysters from Ireland have become my favourites.

---

4 servings

2.5 g fresh yeast (a piece the size of
    your thumbnail)

$2\frac{1}{2}$ tbsp beer

125 g/4 oz/$\frac{3}{4}$ cup plain (all-purpose)
    flour

salt

1 egg, separated

5 tsp milk

10 g/$\frac{1}{3}$ oz/2 tsp butter, melted

20 fresh oysters

oil for deep frying

fresh flat-leaf parsley, to garnish

FOR THE SAUCE

1 hard-boiled egg, finely chopped

1 tbsp finely chopped capers

2 tbsp finely chopped gherkins

1 tbsp finely chopped fresh flat-leaf
    parsley

1 tbsp finely chopped fresh
    tarragon

2 tsp finely chopped fresh chervil

120 g/4 oz/$\frac{1}{2}$ cup mayonnaise

$\frac{1}{4}$ lemon

Put the yeast in a small bowl and add just enough of the beer to dissolve it. Sift the flour and a pinch of salt into another bowl and make a well in the centre. Put in the yeast mixture, egg yolk, milk and remaining beer. Mix to a smooth batter. Add the butter. Leave the batter at room temperature for 15–20 minutes.

To make the sauce, combine all the ingredients and mix well.

Open the oysters and remove from the shells. Drain in a colander, then lay out on a kitchen cloth or paper towels so excess liquid will be absorbed.

Whisk the egg white until it is stiff, then fold it into the batter. Drop the oysters into the batter.

Heat oil for deep frying until it is very hot. Test the temperature by dropping in a bit of batter; it should rise to the surface immediately and the oil should bubble around it.

Pick up the oysters from the batter one at a time with a fork and fry them in the oil until they are crisp and golden all over. Drain on paper towels. Quickly deep fry some flat-leaf parsley and drain.

Put the sauce in 4 ramekins and set one in the centre of each plate. Surround with the oyster fritters, with a cocktail stick in each one. Garnish with deep-fried parsley and serve immediately.

● All the ingredients for the batter should be at room temperature.

Bruno's notes

● Do not overfill the pan with oil – two-thirds full is the maximum.

● You have to be pretty quick when frying oysters. Be sure to have a plate with paper towels ready nearby to remove excess oil from the fritters.

● The parsley must be completely dry before adding it to the hot oil, otherwise the oil will spit. It will take only 10 seconds to get the parsley crisp.

Salmon and Oyster Purse on a Watercress Salad

Bourse d'Huîtres et Saumon Fumé sur Salade de Cresson

4 servings

2 bunches of watercress

8 fresh oysters

1 tbsp whole-grain mustard

1 tbsp red wine vinegar

about 5 tbsp olive oil

80 g/3 oz shallots, very finely chopped

a piece of salmon fillet, weighing 400 g/14 oz

freshly ground pepper

Preheat the oven to 180°C/350°F/Gas 4.

Pull large stalks from the watercress. Rinse the leaves well in a bowl of cold water, then drain and pat dry.

Open the oysters and remove them from their shells. Strain the liquor from the shells through a fine sieve or strainer lined with muslin or cheesecloth.

In a small bowl, mix together the oyster liquor, mustard, vinegar, 3 tablespoons oil and the shallots. Set this dressing aside.

Slice the salmon horizontally into 4 large escalopes that are about 3 mm/ $\frac{1}{8}$ inch thick. Lay a salmon escalope flat on the work surface and arrange 2 oysters on top. Season with pepper, then wrap up like an old-fashioned coin purse and turn upside-down on an oiled baking tray, tucking in the loose ends. Make 3 more purses in the same way. Brush them with olive oil and bake for 3–4 minutes.

Meanwhile, toss the watercress in the dressing and pile in the centre of the plates. Put the salmon purses on top. Grind some pepper over each purse and drizzle a few drops of olive oil around.

Mussels Cooked on a Pine Board with Pine Needes

Eclade de Moules

Mussels are wonderful, so full of flavour. When I was young we often had them for lunch. Sometimes when my mother brought back the mussels from the fishmonger, we could not wait for the long preparation of mussels in tomato rice, so we would put a few on the stove top. After a minute, they would open and we would eat them, without any seasoning or condiment. This is one of my most pleasurable food memories.

The mussel recipe here is extremely simple but nevertheless very interesting. It comes from Charente Maritime.

---

2 kg/4½ lb very fresh mussels, well
   scrubbed
a piece of pine wood

dry pine needles
freshly ground black pepper

4 servings

Arrange the mussels, large side down, on the pine board. Cover them with the pine needles.

Place the board on the barbecue (outdoors, of course!) and light the needles. When they are all consumed, the mussel shells should be open. Blow away the ashes and serve the mussels, with freshly ground pepper.

● This dish is good fun. It will definitely impress your guests. Prepare it while they enjoy their aperitifs – it will replace the usual boring canapés with style!　**Bruno's note**

Potted Shrimps Bistrot Bruno

Crevettes Grises Bistrot Bruno

In October 1993, Michel Lorain, Michelin three-star chef in France and consultant chef at the Meridien Hotel in London, and my friend David Chambers, then executive chef at the Meridien, asked me to prepare a menu of English food for a special evening at the hotel. The request was quite unusual, and I worked hard to select English dishes that would not be out of place in such a famous French restaurant.

For the first course I came up with potted shrimps, but done somewhat differently from the classic version. I changed the usual clarified butter to a butter flavoured with oysters and anchovies, with a squeeze of lemon to bring up the flavours of the sea. The dish was such a success that I decided to serve it at the Bistrot.

---

4 servings

50 g/1¾ oz/3½ tbsp soft butter

1 tbsp soured cream

2 canned anchovy fillets

2 fresh oysters, removed from their shells

½ lemon

Tabasco sauce

salt and freshly ground pepper

200 g/7 oz cooked peeled small shrimps

⅓ cucumber

1 tbsp olive oil

1 tsp chopped fresh dill

toast or brown bread, to serve

Combine the butter, soured cream, anchovies and oysters in a blender or food processor. Add a squeeze of lemon juice, a drop of Tabasco and some freshly ground pepper. Process until the mixture is smooth.

Put the shrimps in a bowl and add the flavoured butter. Mix well. Line the bottoms of 4 small ramekins with discs of greaseproof (wax) paper. Divide the shrimp mixture among the ramekins and press in smoothly. Loosen from the side of the ramekins with a knife, then turn out the moulded potted shrimps on to the centre of 4 plates. Discard the paper discs. Set aside in a cool place.

Peel the cucumber, cut in half lengthways and remove the seeds with a small spoon. Cut each half across into thin slices. Sprinkle the cucumber slices with salt and leave to drain for 10 minutes, then rinse well and pat dry with paper towels.

Toss the cucumber slices with the oil, remaining lemon juice and the chopped dill. Arrange around the potted shrimps. Serve with toast or bread.

● You can do all the preparation in advance. Take the potted shrimps out of the fridge about 20 minutes before serving. **Bruno's note**

Fresh Tuna Tartare with Tomato and Avocado

Tartare de Thon, Salade de Tomate et Avocat

---

400 g/14 oz very fresh boneless tuna	2 tsp tamari (strong, rich soy sauce) **4 servings**
$\frac{1}{2}$ tbsp chopped capers	1 garlic clove, very finely chopped to a purée
4 spring onions (scallions), chopped	3 tbsp olive oil
$\frac{1}{2}$ tbsp Dijon mustard	$\frac{1}{4}$ lemon
2 tsp chopped fresh coriander (cilantro)	salt and freshly ground pepper
	4 medium-large round tomatoes
4 tsp soured cream	1 avocado

Cut the tuna into very small cubes, about 4 mm/$\frac{1}{8}$ inch. Put into a bowl and add the capers, spring onions, mustard, coriander, soured cream, tamari, garlic, 1 tablespoon of oil and a squeeze of lemon juice. Season with salt and pepper. Mix well, then cover tightly and place in the refrigerator. Slit an 'x' in the skin at the base of each tomato. Immerse them in boiling water and leave for 8 seconds, then remove and plunge into iced water to cool quickly. Drain and peel them. Cut a lid off the top of each tomato and empty the inside. Season with salt. Turn upside down on paper towels to drain for a few minutes.

Fill the tomatoes with the tuna tartare and replace the lids. Set a tomato on each plate.

Peel the avocado and cut it lengthwise into quarters. Cut each quarter across into thin slices. Toss the slices gently in the remaining olive oil and lemon juice with a little salt. Arrange the avocado slices tightly, and slightly overlapping, around the tomatoes and serve.

Bruno's notes	● Make sure you have a bowl of iced water ready before you start to blanch the tomatoes.
	● All the ingredients can be prepared in advance except the avocado.

Baby Squid Salad Bordelaise

This recipe is not a traditional one. I call it *bordelaise* because I've added a red wine reduction to the dressing, which gives more depth of flavour to the dish.

Salade de Calamar Bordelaise

4 servings

200 ml/7 fl oz good red wine,
  preferably Bordeaux
1 tbsp red wine vinegar
6 tbsp olive oil
salt and freshly ground black
  pepper
2 pinches of sugar
600 g/1¼ lb baby squid

1 tbsp chopped fresh flat-leaf
  parsley
2 garlic cloves, chopped
1 tbsp chopped shallot
1 curly endive (frisé)
1 'Little Gem' lettuce (romaine
  heart)
1 bunch of watercress, stalks
  removed

Bring the wine to the boil in a small pan and boil until reduced to about 3 tablespoons. Remove from the heat and leave to cool, then mix in the vinegar and 4 tablespoons olive oil. Season with salt and pepper and add the sugar. Set aside.

Clean the squid. Slit the bodies open. Heat the remaining olive oil in a frying pan and quickly fry the squid bodies and tentacles until they are white and opaque, stirring and tossing. Add the parsley, garlic and shallot and season with salt and pepper. Remove from the heat and keep warm.

Arrange the endive, lettuce and watercress leaves on 4 plates. Place the squid on top. Drizzle with the dressing and finish with a grinding of black pepper.

- Take care when you cook the squid. The pan must be very hot and the squid cooked   **Bruno's notes**
  very quickly and briefly – if cooked too much they will become very chewy.
- Try to get fresh squid rather than using frozen. Fresh squid will not shrink as much as
  frozen and the flavour really is different.

Snails with Tomato Relish and Herb Oil

Escargots au Relish de Tomate, Huile aux Herbes

---

2 tbsp olive oil

60 g/2 oz/$\frac{1}{4}$ cup finely chopped
  onion

2 celery stalks, finely chopped

1 tsp brown sugar

1 garlic clove, finely chopped

$3\frac{1}{2}$ tbsp red wine vinegar

1 tsp tomato paste

1 can (400 g/14 oz) chopped plum
  tomatoes

$\frac{1}{2}$ dried bay leaf

1 sprig of fresh thyme

salt and freshly ground pepper

24 canned Burgundy snails or
    32 grey snails (*petit gris*)

4 large handfuls of mixed salad
  leaves

olive oil dressing (page 205)

herb oil (page 203) to finish

4 servings

Heat the oil in a heavy saucepan and cook the onion and celery for 3–4 minutes, stirring. Add the sugar, garlic and vinegar and mix well. Boil to reduce the liquid completely, then add the tomato paste. Cook, stirring, for 2 minutes. Add the plum tomatoes with their juice, the bay leaf and thyme. Leave to simmer gently for 30 minutes, stirring occasionally.

Season the tomato relish with salt and pepper. Add the snails and heat for 10 minutes. Dress the salad leaves with a little olive oil dressing. Put a bouquet of salad leaves in the centre of each plate. Spoon the snails in tomato relish around the salad. Using a spoon, add a few drops of herb oil around the snails and then finish with a grinding of black pepper. Serve immediately.

Gardener's Snails

Escargots en Jardinière

4 servings	100 g/$3\frac{1}{2}$ oz carrots	150 ml/5 fl oz chicken stock
	100 g/$3\frac{1}{2}$ oz bulb fennel	5 spring onions (scallions), chopped
	150 g/5 oz leeks, white and pale green parts	100 g/$3\frac{1}{2}$ oz/7 tbsp butter, cut into small pieces
	100 g/$3\frac{1}{2}$ oz courgettes (zucchini)	250 g/9 oz plum-type tomatoes,
	100 g/$3\frac{1}{2}$ oz turnips	peeled, seeded and diced
	3 tbsp olive oil	1 tbsp chopped fresh basil
	1 garlic clove, chopped	2 tbsp chopped fresh chives
	150 ml/5 fl oz dry white wine	$\frac{1}{2}$ lemon
	24 canned Burgundy snails or 32 grey snails (*petit gris*)	salt and freshly ground pepper

Cut the carrots, fennel, leeks, courgettes and turnips into 5 mm/$\frac{1}{4}$ inch dice. Heat the olive oil in a saucepan and add the diced vegetables and garlic. Cook over low heat, stirring, for 3–5 minutes or until the vegetables begin to soften. Add the white wine and snails. Bring to the boil and boil to reduce the liquid by half.

Pour in the chicken stock and bring back to the boil. Cook for 1 minute. Add the spring onions, butter, tomatoes and herbs. Tilt the pan to melt and swirl the butter into the sauce. Add a squeeze of lemon juice and salt and pepper to taste. Serve immediately.

● Connoisseurs prefer the smaller *petit gris* snails, considering them to have a more **Bruno's note** refined taste than the larger Burgundy snails. But both are delicious prepared this way.

Hot Goat's Cheese on Grilled Vegetables with Figs

Chèvre Chaud sur Légumes Grillés et Figues

In French bistrots, hot goat's cheese on a garden salad with croûtons is quite a common dish. In my version I have replaced the salad with grilled vegetables and figs, and the croûtons with almonds.

---

		4 servings
2 firm goat's cheeses such as *Crottin de Chavignole*, each weighing about 60 g/2 oz	100 ml/$3\frac{1}{2}$ fl oz olive oil	
2 tbsp flour	2 tsp balsamic vinegar	
1 egg, lightly beaten	150 g/5 oz aubergine (eggplant)	
4 tbsp nibbed almonds	salt	
2 red sweet peppers	100 g/$3\frac{1}{2}$ oz courgettes (zucchini)	
4 tbsp water	2 purple figs	
	1 tbsp chopped fresh basil	
	2 garlic cloves, chopped	

Cut the goat's cheeses in half horizontally. Coat them lightly with flour, then dip in beaten egg and coat with almonds. Put aside in the refrigerator.

Preheat the oven to 200°C/400°F/Gas 6.

Place the sweet peppers in a small roasting pan with the water and 2 tablespoons of the oil. Cover with foil and roast for about 10 minutes.

Lift the peppers into a bowl and cover tightly; reserve the juices in the pan. After about 5 minutes the peppers should be cool enough to handle; remove the skin and seeds. Add the juices from the peppers to those in the pan. Stir in the vinegar. Set aside.

Preheat the grill (broiler) to high.

Cut the aubergine lengthwise into slices 1 cm/$\frac{3}{8}$ inch thick. Sprinkle with salt and set aside.

Cut the courgettes lengthwise into slices 5–7 mm/about $\frac{1}{4}$ inch thick. Toss in olive oil, season with salt and grill until lightly browned and just tender. Repeat the operation with the seeded peppers and aubergine.

Cut the figs vertically into 5 mm/$\frac{1}{4}$ inch slices. Place under the hot grill for 2 minutes, then add them to the vegetables with the basil and garlic. Keep warm.

Heat a film of oil in a frying pan and pan-fry the cheeses to colour both sides. Transfer carefully to a baking sheet and finish the cooking in the hot oven, about 3 minutes.

Meanwhile, spoon the vegetables into the centre of the warmed plates and surround with a ring of the pepper juice mixture. Add a few drops of olive oil and place the cheese on top. Serve immediately.

Bruno's notes

- You can also use 4 slices from a log-shaped goat's cheese.
- If you have a charcoal grill available, grill the vegetables to mark both sides attractively, then transfer to a frying pan to finish the cooking if necessary.
- You can serve this dish as a main course, with a green salad, in which case double the quantity of cheese.

Poached Egg on Onion and Red Wine Purée

Oeuf Poché, Purée d'Oignon au Vin Rouge

115 g/4 oz/$\frac{1}{2}$ cup butter or duck fat

1 kg/2$\frac{1}{4}$ lb onions, thinly sliced

salt and freshly ground pepper

2 garlic cloves, sliced

500 ml/16 fl oz red wine

8 very fresh free-range eggs

vinegar

1 tbsp chopped fresh flat-leaf
  parsley

4 servings

Melt three-quarters of the butter or duck fat in a pan. Add the onions and season with salt and pepper. Cook gently until the onions start to soften, stirring frequently. Add the garlic and red wine and bring to the boil. Reduce the heat and cook slowly until only 4 tablespoons of liquid are left.

Pour the onion mixture into a blender or food processor and blend until smooth. Pour into a clean pan and add the remaining butter or duck fat. Check the seasoning. Keep hot.

Poach the eggs in a pan of simmering salted water to which a few drops of vinegar have been added. Remove and drain on paper towels.

Spoon the onion and red wine purée on to the centre of each plate and place 2 poached eggs on top of each serving. Sprinkle with the parsley and grind over some pepper.

Warm Leek Salad with Poached Eggs and Lardons

Salade Tiède de Poireau, Oeuf Poché, Lardons

For many years I prepared a dish of leeks pressed in a terrine until all the juices were drained out. The result looked stunning on the plate. Today I would call this dish César, in honour of the famous French sculptor whose works are based on compression. However, in cooking today one must put the natural taste of the ingredients first, not the design. So here I serve the leeks just out of their cooking liquid, to allow all their flavour to come through. The addition of the poached egg yolk adds richness to what is essentially a simple salad.

---

4 servings

800 g/1¾ lb small leeks, white and
    pale green parts

vegetable oil

4 slices of smoked streaky bacon
    (thick bacon slices), cut across
    into *lardons*

4 very fresh free range eggs

vinegar

1 tbsp chopped fresh chervil

FOR THE DRESSING

1 tsp Dijon mustard

1 tbsp red wine vinegar

salt and freshly ground black
    pepper

3 tbsp walnut oil

1 tbsp vegetable oil

Bring a large pan of salted water to the boil. Add the leeks and simmer until they are just tender. The cooking time depends on the size and quality of the leeks (this varies according to the time of year). Test with the point of a sharp knife.

Meanwhile, make the dressing: mix together the mustard, vinegar and some salt and pepper. Gradually whisk in the oils.

Heat a film of vegetable oil in a frying pan and fry the bacon until lightly browned. Drain the *lardons* on paper towels.

Poach the eggs in a pan of simmering salted water to which a few drops of vinegar have been added. Remove and drain on paper towels.

Drain the leeks in a colander, then place on a clean cloth, fold over the sides and gently press out excess water. Toss the leeks in the dressing with the chervil.

Arrange the leeks in the centre of each plate like a nest and set a poached egg on top. Sprinkle with the *lardons* and finish with a grinding of pepper.

● After draining the leeks, do not refresh them in cold water. If they are too hot to handle, you might try wearing rubber gloves! **Bruno's note**

Risotto with Parmesan

Risotto au Parmesan

Along with other mystical dishes such as *beurre blanc* and *brioche*, risotto has a reputation for being very difficult to make. But this isn't true: it only takes a bit of common sense and understanding for the result to be successful. There are three exceptional varieties of Italian rice for making risotto – arborio, vialone and carnavoli. All are good, and arborio is widely available, but my choice would be vialone.

---

900 ml/1½ pints/3¾ cups beef
    bouillon (page 16) or
    250 ml/8 fl oz canned beef
    consommé plus enough water to
    make the bouillon quantity
2 tbsp olive oil
150 g/5 oz onion, finely chopped
1 small garlic clove, finely chopped

350 g/12 oz/1½ cups risotto rice
½ glass of dry white wine
1 small sprig of fresh rosemary
2 tbsp freshly grated Parmesan or
    more to taste
salt and freshly ground black
    pepper
virgin olive oil to serve

4 servings

Before you start the risotto, heat the bouillon in a saucepan until almost boiling. Keep hot.

Pour the oil into a wide heavy pan, add the onion and garlic and cook over moderate heat until the onion is soft, stirring occasionally. Add the rice and stir well to coat the grains with the oil. Add the white wine and simmer until the rice has absorbed it all, stirring constantly.

Add a small ladleful of the hot bouillon and stir well all around the pan and across the bottom to be sure the rice isn't sticking. Cook, stirring constantly, until the bouillon has been absorbed. Add another ladleful of bouillon and repeat the process. Keep adding the bouillon in this way, stirring and cooking. After about 20 minutes cooking, taste a few grains of rice for texture. You may want to cook for another 5 minutes or so.

About 2 or 3 minutes before the rice is ready, add the rosemary and Parmesan. Stir well and season with salt.

Serve in deep soup plates, grinding pepper over the tops. Put a bottle of virgin olive oil on the table so everyone can help themself.

Bruno's notes
- You need to stir risotto constantly during cooking so the starch will be released from the grain, giving the wonderful creamy texture that is characteristic of this dish.
- The Parmesan must be freshly grated – that sold dried and already grated is horrible and is the reason why many people don't like Parmesan.

Chicory, Roquefort and Walnut Salad

Salade d'Endive au Roquefort et Noix

Roquefort, with its strong distinctive flavour and firm yet buttery texture, is to my mind the king of French cheeses. I can remember my family eating Roquefort when I was a little boy, always presenting it with great ceremony. I'd like to think this was due to the incomparable taste of the cheese, but it probably had more to do with its price. Roquefort is an expensive cheese, but it has such an intense flavour that only a little is needed to give great pleasure.

---

1 baguette, about 15 cm/6 inches long

55 g/2 oz/4 tbsp butter

500 g/1 lb 2 oz chicory (Belgian endive)

1 tsp Dijon mustard

$\frac{1}{2}$ tbsp red wine vinegar

salt and freshly ground black pepper

2 tbsp walnut oil

1 tbsp cold water

125 g/4$\frac{1}{2}$ oz Roquefort cheese

60 g/2 oz walnuts, chopped

6 spring onions (scallions), chopped

4 servings

Preheat the grill (broiler).

Slice the baguette thinly and lay the slices on a baking sheet. Spread the slices with butter, then toast under the grill until both sides are golden. Set the croûtons aside.

Cut each chicory in half lengthwise. Cut out the hard core at the base of each half and separate the leaves. Put the leaves in a large bowl.

Mix together the mustard, vinegar and a little salt. When the salt has dissolved, whisk in the oil and water.

Grind some black pepper over the chicory leaves, then crumble the cheese on top. Add the walnuts, spring onions and croûtons. Finally, dribble over the dressing. Toss well at the table and serve immediately.

● Be cautious when adding salt to the dressing because the cheese is very salty. **Bruno's note**

Salade Niçoise

If you were to ask an Englishman or American to name the most famous salad in the world, he would probably say that it could be either Niçoise or Caesar salad. But if you asked a Frenchman, he would definitely answer Salade Niçoise. I love the mixture of ingredients in the Niçoise, but prefer the character of the Caesar dressing. So I have put them together, in an *Entente Cordiale*.

4 servings

200 g/7 oz French (thin green) beans

12 small new potatoes

3 hard-boiled eggs

6 plum-type tomatoes

$\frac{1}{4}$ baguette, thinly sliced

olive oil

1 garlic clove, halved

hearts of 2 round (butterhead) lettuces or 4 'Little Gem' lettuces

24 black olives

200 g/7 oz canned tuna in olive oil, drained and coarsely flaked

8 fresh basil leaves

FOR THE DRESSING

6 anchovy fillets, canned in olive oil, drained

1 tbsp freshly grated Parmesan

1 tsp Worcestershire sauce

2 egg yolks

2 garlic cloves

1 tbsp lemon juice

6 tbsp olive oil

freshly ground pepper

Put all the ingredients for the dressing in a blender and blend until creamy and smooth in texture. Set aside.

Preheat the grill (broiler).

Cook the French beans in plenty of boiling salted water until just tender. Drain and refresh in iced water. Cook the potatoes in boiling salted water until tender. Drain, refresh and cut into quarters. Cut the eggs and tomatoes into quarters.

Arrange the slices of baguette on a baking sheet and brush them with olive oil. Toast under the grill until golden on both sides. Then rub with the garlic clove.

In a large mixing bowl, combine the lettuce, French beans, potatoes, olives and tuna. Add the dressing and toss. Divide among 4 individual salad bowls. Arrange the egg and tomato quarters on top with the *croûtons*. Finish with a sprinkling of basil, cut with scissors, and a grinding of pepper.

Bruno's notes

- In a Caesar salad, the anchovy is in the salad, but I have added it to the dressing here.
- You could use a food processor to make the dressing, but the cuantity is quite small for the food processor bowl. Another alternative is a hand-held blender.

New Potato and Dill Salad Laced with Smoked Herring Sauce

Salade de Pommes Nouvelles à l'Aneth, Crème de Hareng Fumé

---

4 servings

500 g/1 lb 2 oz new potatoes

100 g/3½ oz smoked herring, roughly chopped

4 tbsp Noilly Prat or other dry vermouth

250 ml/8 fl oz double (heavy) cream

½ lemon

salt and freshly ground pepper

1 tsp Dijon mustard

2 tsp red wine vinegar

2 tbsp olive oil

2 tbsp finely chopped onion

1 tbsp chopped fresh dill

1 hard-boiled egg, chopped

Cook the potatoes in boiling salted water until just tender. When they are done, drain them well.

Put the chopped herring in a saucepan with the Noilly Prat and bring to the boil, then pour in the cream. Leave to simmer for 10 minutes. Press through a fine sieve set over a bowl. Add a squeeze of lemon and season with salt and pepper.

In a large bowl mix together the mustard, vinegar and olive oil. Add the potatoes, onion, dill and chopped hard-boiled egg. Season with salt and pepper and mix well.

Divide the potato salad among the plates, placing it in the centre. Spoon the herring sauce around the potato salad and grind some pepper on top.

Bruno's note   ● This is a very simple starter that can be glorified with a bit of caviare mixed into the potatoes or simply spooned on top.

Mille-feuilles of Grilled Asparagus and Parmesan Cracknel on Beef Carpaccio

Dentelle de Parmesan et Asperges en Mille-feuilles, Carpaccio de Boeuf

In my native South-west, green asparagus is very rare, only found on the shelves of specialist shops. The white asparagus with a pink top is the common one in the area. We used to grow this in the family garden, and one of my favourite pastimes was to look for the crack on the surface of the sandy ground, where the pink top of the asparagus would just be appearing.

Regional restaurants and bistrots serve asparagus with mayonnaise or vinaigrette and Bayonne ham.

---

4 servings

400 g/14 oz medium spears of
    green asparagus
120 ml/4 fl oz olive oil
85 g/3 oz Parmesan, freshly grated
salt and freshly ground black
    pepper
300 g/10 oz beef fillet (tenderloin)
    or sirloin steak
$\frac{1}{2}$ lemon
1 tbsp chopped fresh basil

FOR THE SAUCE

4 eggs
4 spring onions (scallions), finely
    chopped
1 garlic clove, very finely chopped
    (optional)
1 tbsp red wine vinegar
100 ml/$3\frac{1}{2}$ fl oz olive oil

Trim the asparagus and peel if necessary. Cook in boiling salted water for 3 minutes or until just tender but still quite firm. Drain and refresh in iced water. When completely cold, drain the asparagus and pat dry on a clean cloth. Set aside.

Add a dash of vinegar to a small pan of simmering salted water, then poach the eggs for the sauce. Drain and refresh in cold water. Drain on paper towels and leave to cool.

Lightly heat a nonstick frying pan that is about 20 cm/8 inches in diameter. Brush with a film of olive oil, then sprinkle in a thin, even layer of Parmesan. Cook for about 2 minutes or until the cheese melts and turns golden. Use a palette knife (metal spatula) to transfer the Parmesan cracknel to paper towels. Repeat to make 8 cracknel in all.

Prepare a charcoal grill.

To finish the sauce, put the poached eggs in a bowl with the remaining ingredients and crush finely with a fork. Season with salt and pepper.

Toss the asparagus in olive oil and season with salt and pepper. Chargrill to mark them on all sides.

Cut the beef into very thin slices. Divide among 4 flat plates, arranging them in one layer if possible, and cover with cling film (plastic wrap). Pound until the beef is very thin. Remove the film and brush the beef with olive oil. Sprinkle with lemon juice and season with sea salt and pepper.

Place a Parmesan cracknel on top of each carpaccio, then add the grilled asparagus and sprinkle with basil. Top with the remaining cracknel. Spoon the egg sauce around and serve.

- This very elegant starter needs to be assembled at the last minute, but all the components can be prepared in advance.
- To test if the asparagus is cooked, cut out a small piece and taste it.

Bruno's notes

Pancetta with French Bean and Roquefort Salad

Salade de Haricot Vert au Roquefort, Pancetta

4 servings

300 g/10 oz French (thin green) beans

2 tsp Dijon mustard

80 g/scant 3 oz Roquefort cheese

1 tbsp red wine vinegar

3 tbsp walnut oil

$3\frac{1}{2}$ tbsp water

3 shallots, chopped

20 thin slices of pancetta

freshly ground black pepper

Blanch the beans in boiling salted water for 2 minutes, keeping them firm and crisp. Drain and immerse in iced water. When completely cold, drain in a colander and pat dry with a clean cloth.

Combine the mustard, cheese, vinegar, walnut oil and water in a blender or food processor and blend until smooth.

Toss the beans in the cheese dressing and add the chopped shallots.

Arrange the bean salad in the centre of the plates, piling the beans up in a criss-cross fashion. Drape the slices of pancetta around the salad and finish with a grinding of pepper. Serve with good country bread.

Lambs' Brains with Salsa Verde

Cervelles d'Agneau, Sauce Verte

---

4 lambs' brains

2 tbsp vinegar

salt and freshly ground black
   pepper

flour for coating

3 tbsp vegetable oil

20 g/$\frac{2}{3}$ oz/4 tsp butter

TO SERVE

hot boiled potatoes, sliced

salsa verde (page 199)

4 servings

Put the brains in a bowl of iced salted water. Leave to soak overnight. Drain.

Bring a saucepan of water to the boil with the vinegar, 1 teaspoon salt and the brains. Simmer for 5 minutes, then drain and refresh under cold running water. With a small knife, trim off all the little bits of coagulated blood from the brains.

Roll the brains in flour to coat lightly all over. Heat a film of vegetable oil in a frying pan, then add the butter. Pan fry the brains over a brisk heat to colour them lightly on both sides, then reduce the heat and continue to cook for 7–8 minutes, turning occasionally.

Place the brains in the centre of the plates, on top of a few slices of boiled potato. Spoon the salsa verde over the brains and serve.

Spaghetti with Onions, Capers, Anchovies and Coriander

Spaghetti aux Oignons, Câpres, Anchois et Coriandre

4 servings

olive oil

400 g/14 oz onions, chopped

12–16 canned anchovy fillets, drained and chopped

1 garlic clove, finely chopped

1 tbsp small capers

2 tsp coriander seeds, finely crushed in a spice mill or with a mortar and pestle

1 tbsp chopped fresh coriander (cilantro)

350 g/12 oz spaghetti

extra virgin olive oil

$\frac{1}{2}$ lemon

freshly ground black pepper

Heat a film of olive oil in a saucepan, add the onions and cook slowly over a gentle heat until very soft. Remove from the heat and add the anchovies, garlic, capers, coriander seeds and chopped fresh coriander. Mix well and set aside.

Cook the spaghetti in a large pan of boiling salted water until it is al dente. This should take 8–10 minutes, but check the package directions (as long as they're not in Italian!).

Drain the spaghetti in a colander, but don't drain completely. Return the pasta to its cooking pot with a little of the cooking water and add the onion and anchovy mixture. Toss together thoroughly.

Divide the spaghetti among warmed plates and dress each serving with a few drops of virgin olive oil, a squeeze of lemon and some freshly ground black pepper. Serve immediately.

Shallot Tarte Tatin with Sautéed Chicken Livers

Tatin d'Echalotte, Foie de Volaille Sauté

4 servings

20 shallots, peeled

500 ml/16 fl oz red wine

1 bay leaf

5 tbsp honey

90 g/3 oz/6 tbsp butter

freshly ground pepper

4 puff pastry discs, each 10 cm/
4 inches in diameter and 2 mm/
$\frac{1}{16}$ inch thick

vegetable oil

350 g/12 oz chicken livers,
trimmed and cut into bite-size
pieces

2 garlic cloves, very finely chopped

100 ml/$3\frac{1}{2}$ fl oz red wine vinegar

1 tbsp chopped blanched flat-leaf
parsley

$\frac{1}{2}$ tbsp chopped fresh chives

Combine the shallots, wine, bay leaf and honey in a saucepan. Bring to the boil, then reduce the heat and leave to simmer for 45 minutes.

Drain the shallots in a colander set in a bowl; set them aside. Pour the red wine through a fine sieve into a clean saucepan and boil until reduced to 4 tablespoons.

Preheat the oven to 220°C/425°F/Gas 7.

Whisk half the butter into the reduced red wine. Season with pepper. Divide equally among 4 tartlet moulds, each about 10 cm/4 inches in diameter. Put 5 shallots close together in the centre of each mould. Cover with the puff pastry discs and gently press the pastry down around the shallots so that it just touches the red wine reduction on the bottom of the moulds.

Arrange the moulds in a baking tray or roasting pan and add a little water to the tray or pan. Bake for about 5 minutes or until the pastry is risen and golden brown.

Meanwhile, heat a film of vegetable oil in a frying pan and add 15 g/

$\frac{1}{2}$ oz / 1 tablespoon of butter. When hot, add the chicken livers and sauté until they are browned all over but still pink in the middle. Add the garlic and vinegar and boil until reduced to one-third. Add the parsley and the remaining butter, cut into small pieces, and tilt the pan to melt the butter and swirl it into the sauce.

Unmould a shallot Tatin in the centre of each plate and arrange the livers and sauce around. Sprinkle over the chives and give a twist of the pepper mill. Serve immediately.

MILLE-FEUILLES OF GRILLED ASPARAGUS AND PARMESAN CRACKNEL ON BEEF CARPACCIO, *PAGE 44*

SHALLOT TARTE TATIN WITH SAUTÉED CHICKEN LIVERS, *PAGE 49*

MAIN COURSES

Fish

The supermarket shelves are a reflection of the aspirations and lifestyle of a country. In Britain the choice and availability of food have improved enormously in the past ten years: herbs, spices, vegetables and cuts of meat are much better quality and much more diverse. However, there still is a long way to go with fish. The British Isles have a rich heritage of fishing, but this is not reflected in the shops and it is a disgrace. Why is it that nobody is complaining, demanding better quality and variety? If people complain, things will improve.

Whole Snappers Baked with Lime Pickle and Coriander

Poisson au four, Citron Vert à l'Oriental et Coriander

Whenever possible, I cook fish on the bone because it retains all its natural moisture and, I think, has more flavour. Unfortunately the fashion of the past few years has been to fillet, cut and slice fish, and even sometimes to purée it to make a horrible little 'sponge' called a mousse.

Following my determination to use food as naturally as possible, I have banned mousses from my kitchen for many years. The only ones made in my restaurant are done with shellfish, which has a strong flavour and the right texture for a mousse.

---

4 servings

4 red snappers, each weighing 500 g/1 lb 2 oz, cleaned

2 tbsp lime pickle

2 garlic cloves, chopped

2 tsp coriander seeds, crushed

100 ml/$3\frac{1}{2}$ fl oz olive oil

salt and freshly ground pepper

200 g/7 oz tomatoes, preferably plum-type, thinly sliced

2 tbsp chopped fresh coriander (cilantro)

$\frac{1}{2}$ lemon

Preheat the oven to 220°C/425°F/Gas 7.

Make 3 incisions on each side of each fish and place them in a shallow roasting pan.

In a small bowl, stir together the lime pickle, garlic, coriander seeds and oil. Season with salt and pepper.

Brush the fish with the lime pickle mixture on both sides. Arrange the tomato slices over the fish. Bake for about 10 minutes. Every 2 minutes, brush with the lime pickle mixture.

Transfer the fish to warmed plates. Sprinkle with the fresh coriander, add a squeeze of lemon and it's ready.

Bruno's notes

- You can use grey bream instead of snapper.
- The fish can be cooked on a barbecue. If so, it should be brushed frequently with the lime pickle mixture.

Poached Skate Wing in Oyster and Green Masala Sauce

Aile de Raie Pochée, Sauce à l'Huître et Curry

The sauce here is very simple to make and it adds a wonderful depth of flavour to poached fish, particularly skate. This dish is representative of my style of cooking, after 12 years in England: simple French techniques combined with oriental spicing and an unusual but well calculated combination of ingredients.

---

4 servings

1.5 litres/$2\frac{1}{3}$ pints/$1\frac{1}{2}$ quarts poaching stock (page 58)

2 skate wings, weighing about 1.5 kg/3 lb 5 oz

2 tbsp double (heavy) cream

2 tsp Thai green masala curry paste

4 freshly shelled oysters with their liquor

60 g/2 oz/4 tbsp soft butter, in pieces

juice of $\frac{1}{4}$ lemon

1 tbsp chopped fresh coriander (cilantro)

salt and freshly ground pepper

Pour the poaching stock into a large wide pan. Put the skate wings into the stock and bring to the boil. Simmer for 3 minutes, then remove from the heat. Remove 150 ml/$\frac{1}{4}$ pint/$\frac{2}{3}$ cup of the stock and put it in a saucepan.

Cover the large pan and leave the fish to finish cooking in the hot liquid, off the heat.

Meanwhile, add the cream and masala paste to the stock in the saucepan and bring to the boil, stirring. Boil for 2 minutes. Leave to cool slightly, then pour into a blender. Add the oysters with their liquor, the butter and lemon juice and blend until smooth. Pass this sauce through a fine sieve into a clean saucepan. Gently reheat the sauce without letting it boil. Stir in the coriander and adjust the seasoning.

Drain the skate wings and cut each in half. Serve with the sauce. Broad bean and lovage purée (page 147) has enough character to 'argue' with this dish.

Bruno's note   ● It is important that you don't hold the sauce after adding the oysters because it will separate.

Fresh Cod Cooked in Chorizo Cream Sauce

Cabillaud à la Crème de Chorizo

100 ml/3½ fl oz dry white wine

300 ml/10 fl oz chicken stock

1 garlic clove, crushed with the side of a knife

200 ml/7 fl oz double (heavy) cream

100 g/3½ oz chorizo, thinly sliced

4 thick pieces of skinned cod fillet, each weighing 160 g/5½ oz

60 g/2 oz/4 tbsp butter, cut into small pieces

1 tbsp red wine vinegar

2 tbsp chopped fresh chives

red kidney bean purée (page 156), to serve

4 servings

Preheat the oven to 200°C/400°F/Gas 6.

In a saucepan, bring the wine to the boil and boil for 1 minute. Add the stock and garlic. Bring back to the boil, then add half of the cream and the chorizo.

Place the pieces of cod in a baking dish and pour over the chorizo mixture. Bake for about 10 minutes.

Transfer the fish to a plate, cover and keep warm. Pour the cooking liquid into a blender and add the remaining cream. Blend for 1 minute, then press through a fine sieve into a clean saucepan. Boil to reduce to a saucelike consistency. Whisk in the butter, a few pieces at a time, then add the vinegar and chives.

Put a spoonful of red kidney bean purée on one side of each plate. Put the fish on the other side and spoon the sauce over. Serve immediately.

● Chorizo is a dry Spanish sausage spiced with pimento. A purée of red kidney beans will complement the fish and sauce perfectly, carrying through the Spanish influence. **Bruno's note**

Fresh Cod Wrapped in Parma Ham, with Roasted Peppers, Garlic and Capers

Cabillaud au Jambon de Parma, Poivrons Rotis, Ail et Câpres

4 servings

4 thick pieces of cod fillet, each
    weighing 160 g/5½ oz
salt and freshly ground pepper
8 very thin slices of Parma ham
olive oil

FOR THE PEPPER STEW

6 red sweet peppers
6 yellow sweet peppers

150 ml/5 fl oz olive oil
3 garlic cloves
1 tbsp capers
1 fresh or 2 dried bay leaves
1 sprig of fresh rosemary
100 ml/3½ fl oz water
1 tbsp chopped fresh basil
1 tbsp balsamic vinegar

Preheat the oven to 200°C/400°F/Gas 6.

Put the peppers in a roasting pan with 100 ml/3½ fl oz of the oil. Roast for 20 minutes. Transfer the peppers to a bowl, cover tightly with cling film (plastic wrap) and leave to cool. Reserve the oil in the pan.

When the peppers are cool enough to handle, peel them, reserving all the juices. Discard the seeds and cut the flesh into large strips.

Put the garlic cloves in a small pan of cold water, bring to the boil and boil for 30 seconds. Drain. Repeat this blanching two more times. Drain well, then mix with the pepper strips, capers, bay leaves and rosemary in a saucepan. Add the reserved oil and pepper juices, the remaining oil and the water. Season with salt and pepper. Bring to simmering point, then leave to stew for about 30 minutes.

Meanwhile, season the pieces of cod with pepper and a little salt. Wrap each piece in 2 slices of Parma ham. Chill for 20 minutes. If necessary, heat the oven again, to the same temperature.

Heat a film of olive oil in a frying pan and seal the pieces of cod on both sides. Transfer them to an oiled baking sheet and bake for about 8 minutes, depending on the thickness of the pieces.

Just before serving, add the basil and basalmic vinegar to the pepper stew. Spoon it on to warmed plates and place the cod on top. Grind some pepper around and it's ready.

Bruno's notes

- Salmon can replace the cod.
- To check the cooking of the fish, insert a thin knife blade and leave it for 5 seconds, then bring it to your lips to feel the heat. If the knife is hot, the fish is ready.
- Serve this dish with a crisp green salad.

Aïoli Provençale

By tradition, Aïoli provençale is a Friday supper dish, and because it is so generous it makes a nice family feast. In Provence it isn't unusual to see 15 people seated around a table laden with gigantic dishes of vegetables and poached salt cod, a couple of bowls overflowing with *petit gris* snails, smaller bowls of the garlic mayonnaise called *aïoli*, and a half dozen bottles of rosé de Provence. This is an ideal dish for a party because everything can be prepared in advance.

8 servings

1 piece of fresh cod cut from the tail end, weighing about 1.6 kg/ $3\frac{1}{2}$ lb

coarse sea salt

olive oil

4 globe artichokes, preferably the small variety called *poivrade*, trimmed

lemon

1 kg/$2\frac{1}{4}$ lb new potatoes

400 g/14 oz French (thin green) beans

500 g/1 lb 2 oz young carrots

2 fennel bulbs, each quartered

400 g/14 oz broccoli florets

8 hard-boiled eggs

150 g/5 oz black olives

FOR THE POACHING STOCK

250 g/9 oz onions, thinly sliced

200 g/7 oz carrots, thinly sliced

1 bunch of fresh thyme

1 fresh or 2 dried bay leaves

1 star anise

2 slices of lemon

200 ml/7 fl oz white wine

2 litres/$3\frac{1}{3}$ pints/2 quarts water

FOR THE AÏOLI

10 garlic cloves

2 raw egg yolks

yolk from 1 hard-boiled egg

$\frac{1}{2}$ tbsp Dijon mustard

250 ml/8 fl oz olive oil

250 ml/8 fl oz vegetable oil

$\frac{1}{2}$ lemon

salt and freshly ground white pepper

1 tbsp Pernod

About 24 hours before serving, salt the cod: use the tip of a sharp knife to make small incisions all over the cod at about 2 cm/$\frac{3}{4}$ inch intervals. Put a pinch of coarse sea salt in each incision, then brush the fish all over with olive oil. Wrap it tightly in cling film (plastic wrap) and refrigerate.

To make the poaching stock, put all the ingredients into a large pot. Bring to the boil, then cover and simmer for 20 minutes. Remove from the heat and leave to cool, still covered.

On the day of serving, put the cod on a rack in a fish kettle or other pot large enough to accommodate it. Cover the fish with the cold poaching stock. Bring to the boil and simmer for 1 minute, then remove from the heat. Leave the fish to cool in the liquid.

Add the artichokes to a pan of boiling salted water with a slice of lemon. Cook for about 20 minutes or until you can pull a leaf out easily. Drain upside down.

Cook the potatoes, beans, carrots, fennel and broccoli individually in boiling salted water until just tender (keep the green vegetables al dente). Drain and refresh in iced water. Set aside.

To make the *aïoli*, cook 9 of the garlic cloves in a small pan of boiling water for about 10 minutes or until soft. Drain and place in a food processor. Add the raw garlic clove, raw and cooked egg yolks and mustard. Process to a smooth purée. With the machine running, gradually pour in the two oils in a slow, steady stream. When all the oil has been added, add the lemon juice and season with salt and pepper. Stir in the Pernod. Spoon the *aïoli* into a bowl, cover tightly and set aside.

When the fish has cooled, remove it carefully from the stock. Peel off the skin. Set the fish in the centre of a large serving dish. Squeeze the juice of half a lemon over and brush with olive oil. Halve the hard-boiled eggs. Arrange the eggs, olives and vegetables around the fish, alternating the colours. To finish, sprinkle with a little sea salt. Serve with the *aïoli*.

Bruno's notes

- If you don't like artichokes, use green asparagus instead.
- If the *aïoli* is too thick, stir in a little of the poaching stock.
- Don't throw away the poaching stock. Strain it, then freeze and use when making fish soup.

Home-made Salted Cod on Minestrone Vegetables

Morue Fraîche en Minestrone

When I started cooking at Gastronome One restaurant in London, the budget was very tight and I was always looking for bargains. At the time cod was unknown on the restaurant scene, with only Dover sole, turbot, lobster and so on appearing on menus. You would only find cod prepared as fish and chips. Today things are different, of course, and cod is extremely popular, but I've always thought that cod was a marvellous fish, and have tried to use it over the years, giving it interesting touches. I do not hesitate to partner it with many different ingredients such as aubergine 'confit', ham, meat sauce and so on. It is an exciting fish to work with.

4 servings

100 g/3$\frac{1}{2}$ oz dried salted cod

4 thick pieces of cod fillet, each weighing about 160 g/5$\frac{1}{2}$ oz

chopped fresh flat-leaf parsley, to garnish

FOR THE MINESTRONE

150 g/5 oz carrots

120 g/4 oz turnips

150 g/5 oz onions

150 g/5 oz celery

100 g/3$\frac{1}{2}$ oz courgettes (zucchini)

100 ml/3$\frac{1}{2}$ fl oz olive oil

2 garlic cloves, chopped

150 g/5 oz Savoy cabbage, chopped

1 sprig of fresh rosemary

120 g/4 oz ripe plum-type tomatoes, peeled and chopped, or you can use drained canned plum tomatoes, chopped

200 g/7 oz/1 cup canned cannellini beans, well drained

1.5 litres/2$\frac{1}{3}$ pints/1$\frac{1}{2}$ quarts water

60 g/2 oz French (thin green) beans, cut into 2 cm/$\frac{3}{4}$ inch pieces

60 g/2 oz spaghetti, broken into 2–3 cm/$\frac{3}{4}$–1$\frac{1}{4}$ inch pieces

60 g/2 oz/4 tbsp butter (optional)

1 tbsp pesto sauce

$\frac{1}{2}$ lemon

salt and freshly ground pepper

The day before, use a knife to scrape the salted cod into small bits and pieces. Chop with a heavy knife until very fine. Set the pieces of cod skin side down and season the top of each with the salted fish. Wrap each portion tightly in cling film (plastic wrap) and keep in the refrigerator overnight.

On the day, prepare the minestrone. Cut the carrots, turnips, onions, celery and courgettes into 1 cm/$\frac{3}{8}$ inch pieces. Heat the olive oil in a large saucepan, add the onions and cook until lightly golden. Add the garlic and mix well, then add the carrots, turnips, celery, cabbage and rosemary. Cook gently for about 5 minutes, stirring from time to time. When all the flavours of the vegetables start to blend together, add the tomatoes and cannellini beans. Pour over the water and bring to the boil. Leave to cook gently for 30 minutes.

Preheat the oven to 150°C/300°F/Gas 2.

Add the courgettes, French beans and pasta to the minestrone. Simmer for a further 10 minutes.

Meanwhile, arrange the cod fillets on a baking sheet or in a roasting pan, skin side down, and bake for about 8 minutes, depending on the thickness of the fish.

Strain the minestrone liquid through a colander set in a bowl. Keep the vegetables and pasta warm and pour the liquid back into the pan. Boil to reduce to about 400 ml/14 fl oz. Transfer to a blender. Add the butter, if using, and the pesto and blend quickly to an emulsion.

Pour the liquid back into the pan again and add the vegetables and pasta. Add a squeeze of lemon and check the seasoning. Reheat briefly if necessary.

Ladle the minestrone into 4 big soup plates. Remove the skin from the fish, then set a fillet in the centre of each plate. Sprinkle with parsley and serve.

Bruno's notes

- It is important to marinate the fish overnight to allow the flesh to absorb the salt and dried fish flavour. The beauty of this dish is to have the particular taste of the salted fish and the flakiness of the fresh one.
- Lay your table with a fork, knife and soup spoon for each setting.
- Rather than adding butter to the minestrone liquid, you could finish each serving with a few drops of olive oil.

Smoked Haddock Cooked in Milk, Potato and Leek Broth

Haddock Poché au Lait, Pomme de Terre et Poireaux

4 servings

600 g/1 lb 5 oz leeks

800 g/1¾ lb potatoes

500 ml/16 fl oz milk

2 garlic cloves, chopped

salt and freshly ground pepper

4 pieces of smoked haddock fillet
(finnan haddie), each weighing
150 g/5 oz

2 tbsp roughly chopped fresh flat-
leaf parsley

½ lemon

Trim and chop the leeks. Peel the potatoes and cut into 1.5 cm/½ inch pieces. Place in a saucepan and cover with the milk. Add the garlic, season with salt and pepper and bring to the boil. Leave to cook at simmering point for 1 hour.

Put the fish in the pan and cook over low heat for 5 minutes.

Just before serving, add the parsley and a squeeze of lemon.

Bruno's note

● An old wives' trick is to marinate the haddock in plain yogurt. This makes the fish very moist. Rinse it well and pat dry before placing it in the cooking liquid.

Crispy Mackerel, Chilli and Herb Sauce

Maquereaux Croustillant, Sauce Herbes et Chili

4 tbsp honey

3 tbsp red wine vinegar

2 tbsp dark soy sauce

8 fresh mackerel fillets

flour for coating

vegetable oil

3 tbsp sesame seeds

freshly cooked pasta, to serve

FOR THE SAUCE

1 tbsp chopped fresh mint

1 tbsp chopped fresh basil

1 tbsp chopped fresh coriander
  (cilantro)

2 tbsp chopped fresh flat-leaf
  parsley

$\frac{1}{2}$ tsp chopped fresh hot green chilli
  pepper

1 garlic clove

200 ml/7 fl oz olive oil

4 tbsp plain yogurt

salt

4 servings

Put the honey, vinegar and soy sauce in a small pan and boil to reduce by two-thirds. Set aside.

Combine all the sauce ingredients in a blender and blend until smooth. Season with salt only.

Preheat the grill (broiler).

Dust the skin of the fish fillets with flour. Heat a film of vegetable oil in a frying pan and quickly fry the fish, on the skin side only, until golden.

Transfer the fish to a metal dish or tray, placing it skin side up. Spoon the honey mixture over the skin and sprinkle with sesame seeds. Place under the grill and cook until nicely coloured.

Serve 2 fillets on each warmed plate, with fresh pasta. Spoon the sauce over the pasta and serve.

Mackerel Kebab with Piccalilli, Potato Cake and Lettuce

Brochette de Maquereaux sur Piccalilli, Gâteau de Pomme, Laitue

Mackerel is an oily-fleshed fish found in the Mediterranean and in the Atlantic and Pacific Oceans. It is widely available all year round. Many people do not realize how good mackerel is, and how nutritious – it certainly doesn't deserve its down market reputation. To be honest, it is my favourite fish, and I often have it on my menu at the Bistrot.

4 servings

8 fresh mackerel fillets

salt and freshly ground pepper

olive oil

$\frac{1}{2}$ lemon

4 potato cakes (page 133)

$\frac{1}{2}$ Iceberg lettuce, roughly shredded

lemon dressing (page 205)

FOR THE PICCALILLI

4 tbsp olive oil

150 g/5 oz carrots, diced

1 red sweet pepper, seeded and diced

150 g/5 oz fennel bulb, diced

150 g/5 oz celery, diced

150 g/5 oz onions, finely chopped

200 g/7 oz tiny cauliflower florets

1 bay leaf

2 garlic cloves, finely chopped

1 tsp finely chopped fresh ginger

1 tsp turmeric

$\frac{1}{2}$ tsp curry powder

100 ml/$3\frac{1}{2}$ fl oz white wine

1 tsp sugar

200 ml/7 fl oz water

3 tbsp white wine vinegar

100 g/$3\frac{1}{2}$ oz courgettes (zucchini), diced

1 tbsp cornflour (cornstarch) mixed with 3 tbsp water

1 tbsp coarse-grain mustard

$\frac{1}{2}$ tbsp chopped fresh coriander (cilantro)

Cut the mackerel fillets into 3 cm/$1\frac{1}{4}$ inch pieces. Season them with salt and pepper. Thread on to bamboo or metal skewers and brush lightly with oil. Keep in the refrigerator until ready to cook.

To make the piccalilli, heat the oil in a saucepan and add the carrots, red pepper, fennel, celery, onions and cauliflower. Stir with a wooden spoon for a few minutes, then add the bay leaf, garlic, ginger, turmeric, curry powder and white wine. Season with salt and pepper and add the sugar. Pour in the water and vinegar and bring to the boil. Simmer for 5 minutes, then add the courgettes and cook for 2 minutes longer.

Gradually stir in the cornflour mixture, adding just enough to thicken the liquid to the right consistency. Stir in the mustard and cook for a final 2 minutes. Add the chopped coriander, mix well and pour on to a plate. Leave to cool.

Prepare a charcoal fire. Preheat the oven to 220°C/425°F/Gas 7.

Grill the mackerel kebabs over the hot coals to seal and brown lightly on all sides. Transfer them to a roasting pan and squeeze some lemon juice over them. Finish by cooking in the oven for a few minutes.

Spoon some piccalilli on one side of each plate and place the kebabs on top. Add a potato cake and a bit of lettuce tossed in lemon dressing to each plate and serve immediately.

● If more convenient, you can cook the kebabs on a cast iron ridged grill pan.   **Bruno's note**

Salmon Fillet with Peas, Thyme and Smoked Bacon Sauce

Filet de Saumon, Sauce Petit Pois, Thym et Bacon Fumé

I've been asked many times where my ideas come from. It's a difficult question to answer – like asking a composer the source of his musical inspiration – but for me it's the intrinsic flavours and textures of different foods and experimenting with combining them. The recipe here is a good example:

smoked bacon, peas and thyme are not unfamiliar or exotic ingredients, but blending them together to make a tasty and simple sauce for fish is more unusual. The basis for this is found in classic cuisine; this is my interpretation.

4 servings

85 g/3 oz/6 tbsp butter

4 rashers of smoked streaky bacon (thick bacon slices), cut across into *lardons*

100 g/3½ oz leeks, finely chopped

1 sprig of fresh thyme

300 ml/10 fl oz chicken stock or water

200 g/7 oz frozen petit pois, thawed

salt and freshly ground black pepper

olive oil

650 g/1 lb 7 oz salmon fillet, cut into 4 pieces

spinach with almonds and nutmeg (page 142), to serve

Melt 30 g/1 oz/2 tablespoons of the butter in a saucepan. Add the bacon, leeks and thyme and cook gently, stirring, until the leeks are soft. Add the stock or water and bring to the boil. Cook for 10 minutes. Add the peas and cook for a further 10 minutes.

Pour the pea and bacon mixture into a blender or food processor and process until smooth. Pass through a fine sieve set over a clean saucepan. Reheat the sauce. Add the remaining butter, in small pieces, and tilt the pan to melt the butter and swirl it into the sauce. Taste and add salt and pepper (be careful with the salt because the bacon may be salty). Keep the sauce warm.

Heat a film of olive oil in a non-stick frying pan. Add the pieces of salmon fillet and pan-fry for 3 minutes on each side.

Make a bed of spinach in the centre of each plate and set a piece of salmon fillet on top. Spoon the sauce around and serve.

Grilled Salmon Escalopes with Tomato and Anchovy Sauce

Saumon Grillé, Coulis de Tomate à l'Huile d'Anchois

450 g/1 lb ripe plum-type tomatoes	freshly ground black pepper	**4 servings**
6 canned anchovy fillets	125 ml/4 fl oz olive oil, plus more	
1 garlic clove, crushed with the side	for brushing the salmon	
of a knife	4 salmon escalopes, each weighing	
1 tsp Dijon mustard	150 g/5 oz	
1 tbsp red wine vinegar	smooth broccoli purée (page 141)	

Cut the tomatoes in half and squeeze out the seeds. Chop the tomatoes roughly and put them in a blender or food processor. Add the anchovies with their oil, the garlic, mustard, vinegar and some black pepper. Blend until smooth. Add $5\frac{1}{2}$ tablespoons of the oil and blend again. Push the sauce through a fine sieve set over a saucepan. Set the sauce aside

Prepare a charcoal fire or preheat a ridged cast iron grill pan.

Warm the sauce, but don't let it get too hot.

Meanwhile brush the salmon escalopes with oil. Lay them on the grill over hot coals or on the hot grill pan and cook for 2 minutes on each side.

Spoon the broccoli purée in the centre of each plate and set a salmon escalope on top. Spoon the warm sauce around and add a dash of fresh olive oil. Serve quickly.

- When pan-grilling the salmon escalopes, lay them on the hot pan and cook for 1 minute, then lift them carefully and give them a quarter turn. Cook for another minute, then turn the escalopes over and cook the other sides in the same way. This will give the escalopes attractive criss-cross marks. If using a barbecue, you may want to put the salmon in a hinged wire basket to make turning easier.
- Try not to overheat the tomato and anchovy sauce or it will lose its fresh flavour.
- Serve with a green salad or a vegetable such as ratatouille (page 146).

Glazed Salmon Confit on Butter Beans

Escalope de Saumon Confit, Ragout de Haricot Blanc

In a confit, meat such as duck, goose, pork and sometimes chicken is cooked in its own fat. Here, I have given the confit treatment to fish, cooking salmon in duck fat. The flavours of the fish and fat complement each other very well.

4 servings

100 g/3½ oz celery

150 g/5 oz onions

150 g/5 oz carrots

500 ml/16 fl oz duck fat

1 bouquet garni (page 209)

120 g/4 oz dried butter beans, soaked overnight and drained

700–900 ml/1¼–1⅔ pints/3–4 cups chicken stock

4 pieces of salmon fillet, each weighing 120 g/4 oz

1 tbsp chopped blanched flat-leaf parsley

1 garlic clove, chopped

sea salt and freshly ground black pepper

FOR THE GLAZE

1 tbsp tomato ketchup

1 tsp tomato paste

2 tsp Worcestershire sauce

1 tbsp honey

1 garlic clove, finely chopped

2 tsp finely chopped fresh ginger

3 tbsp malt vinegar

Cut the celery, onions and carrots into 1 cm/$\frac{3}{8}$ inch dice. Heat 3 tablespoons of the duck fat in a large heavy-based saucepan. Add the diced vegetables and bouquet garni and cook for a few minutes, stirring, without letting the vegetables brown. Add the beans and enough stock to cover. Bring to simmering point, then leave to cook for about 2 hours or until the beans are tender, adding more stock as needed.

Heat the remaining duck fat in a wide pan until it is melted and just warm. Add the pieces of salmon and remove from the heat. Leave for about 15 minutes or until the salmon is just cooked.

Meanwhile make the glaze: put all the ingredients in a saucepan and bring to the boil. Reduce, stirring occasionally, until you obtain a thick mixture.

Preheat the grill (broiler).

Remove the salmon from the duck fat and drain it cn paper towels. Arrange the pieces on a baking tray or shallow baking dish and brush them with the glaze. Place under the grill for a few minutes.

Discard the bouquet garni from the beans, and stir in the parsley and garlic. Season to taste. Divide the beans among the plates and set a piece of glazed salmon confit on top of each serving.

- Cooking salmon in duck fat makes the fish very succulent. The duck fat must not be too hot or the outside of the salmon will cook too quickly and will be dry. **Bruno's notes**
- To blanch the parsley, drop the whole sprigs or leaves into boiling water and boil for 30 seconds. Drain and refresh in iced water, then pat dry.

Pan-fried John Dory with Rosemary and Orange 'Gastrique'

St Pierre Poelé, Gastrique à l'Orange et Romarin

A *gastrique* is, basically, a light caramel deglazed with vinegar. For the sauce here I've added orange and rosemary for flavouring, with a bit of butter to soften their assertiveness. The combination may seem unusual with fish, but it works very well, and is typical of the spontaneity of the people of the South of France.

---

4 servings

4 garlic cloves, very thinly sliced

4 john dory, each weighing about
   450 g/1 lb, cleaned and trimmed

salt and freshly ground pepper

flour

olive oil

85 g/3 oz/7 tbsp sugar

150 ml/5 fl oz red wine vinegar

4 small sprigs of fresh rosemary

4 small strips of orange zest

50 g/$1\frac{2}{3}$ oz/$3\frac{1}{2}$ tbsp butter, cut into
   pieces

Preheat the oven to 220°C/425°F/Gas 7.

Put the garlic into a small saucepan, cover with water and bring to the boil. Boil for 2 minutes, then drain and refresh in cold water. Set aside.

Rinse the fish well and pat dry with paper towels. Salt the fish and coat lightly with flour, tapping off the excess.

Heat a film of olive oil in a frying pan. Add two of the fish and cook over high heat to brown lightly on both sides. Then reduce the heat to moderate and cook for a further 4 minutes on each side.

Meanwhile, prepare the sauce. Put the sugar into a heavy saucepan and melt it, then cook until it is golden in colour. Pour in the vinegar and stir well. Bring to the boil. Remove from the heat and add the rosemary, orange zest and garlic. Set aside.

Remove the fried fish to an ovenproof dish and cover with foil. Pan-fry the remaining two fish in the same way and add to the ovenproof dish. Put the dish, uncovered, into the oven and finish cooking the fish for 3–4 minutes.

Reheat the sauce. Add the butter and tilt the pan to melt the butter and swirl it into the sauce. Season with salt and pepper.

Serve the fish on hot plates with the sauce spooned over. Lyonnaise potatoes (page 136) are perfect with this.

● Choose small john dory for this dish – they are much cheaper than the larger ones **Bruno's note** and are perfect to pan-fry on the bone.

Mussels and Lentils in Spicy Pot

Moules et Lentilles à l'Etouffé

In 1235 an Irish sailor named Patrick Walton was shipwrecked north of La Rochelle. Nobody was living around there at the time, and to feed himself he had the idea of placing a net on poles in the water. Some mussels stuck to the poles, and he was hungry enough to try them. Finding them delicious, he decided to improve his trap and so placed some board between the poles. This was the beginning of the system of mussel farming called *bouchot*.

I call this a 'pot' because everything is put in together. There is no separate cooking, so it is a very easy dish to make.

---

4 servings

200 g/7 oz carrots

200 g/7 oz onions

250 g/9 oz celery

85 g/3 oz/6 tbsp butter

200 g/7 oz smoked streaky bacon (thick bacon slices), cut into *lardons*

1 bay leaf

$\frac{1}{2}$–1 fresh hot red chilli pepper, finely chopped

6 green cardamom pods, crushed with the side of a knife

2 tsp curry powder

600 g/1 lb 5 oz/3 cups green lentils

4 garlic cloves, chopped

1.6 kg/$3\frac{1}{2}$ lb very fresh mussels

sea salt

2 tbsp chopped fresh flat-leaf parsley

2 tbsp chopped fresh coriander (cilantro)

Cut the carrots, onions and celery into 1 cm/$\frac{3}{8}$ inch pieces. In a thick-based pan, melt the butter and add the bacon, carrots, onions, celery, bay leaf, chilli, crushed cardamom and curry powder. Stir with a wooden spoon until the vegetables are lightly coloured.

Add the lentils and garlic. Pour over enough water to come about 2 cm/$\frac{3}{4}$ inch above the level of the ingredients. Bring to simmering point, then cover and leave to cook gently for about 40 minutes.

Prepare the mussels by rubbing them with sea salt and then rinse them under cold running water. Place them in a basin of cold water and throw away any that rise to the surface: these are dead. Drain off the water and set the mussels aside in a cool place.

About 10 minutes before the lentils are ready, add the mussels to the pot. Stir, then cover and bring back to simmering point. Remove from the heat and leave to rest for 5 minutes.

Add the parsley and coriander. Check the seasoning and serve.

Risotto of Mussels, Tomatoes and Bacon

Risotto de Moules à la Tomate et Bacon

---

4 servings

150 ml/5 fl oz olive oil, plus extra
  for serving
600 g/1 lb 5 oz very ripe plum-type
  tomatoes, roughly chopped
4 garlic cloves, chopped
200 g/7 oz smoked streaky bacon
  (thick bacon slices), diced
200 g/7 oz onions, chopped

300 g/10 oz/1$\frac{1}{3}$ cups risotto rice
  (arborio)
100 ml/3$\frac{1}{2}$ fl oz white wine
1 litre/1$\frac{2}{3}$ pints/1 quart chicken
  stock
1.6 kg/3$\frac{1}{2}$ lb very fresh mussels,
  scrubbed
2 tbsp chopped fresh flat-leaf
  parsley

In a large pan, heat 100 ml/3½ fl oz of the oil. When it is quite hot, but before any smoke appears, add the tomatoes, garlic and bacon and stir well. Cover and leave to stew for 30 minutes.

Meanwhile, heat the remaining oil in a thick-based pan and cook the onions for 2 minutes. Add the rice and stir with a wooden spoon for a further minute. When the rice becomes shiny, add the wine. Simmer until the rice has absorbed all the wine, then add about one-quarter of the stock. Stir constantly until almost all this stock has been absorbed, then add another quarter of the stock. Repeat, adding the rest of the stock in two batches. This operation should take approximately 15 minutes.

About 5 minutes before the rice is ready, add the mussels to the tomato sauce. Bring to the boil, cover again and cook for 5 minutes.

Add the mussels in tomato sauce to the risotto and mix well. Serve in soup plates, sprinkling each portion with chopped parsley, a few drops of olive oil and some freshly ground pepper.

● If possible, you should stir the risotto constantly while it is cooking. This will produce a very creamy result, as the stirring encourages the rice to give up its starch to the liquid.   **Bruno's note**

Buckwheat Crêpes Filled with Leeks, Mussels, Cockles and Crab

Crêpe au Siegle Fourré de Poireaux, Moules, Coques et Crabe

Here is a dish very popular in Brittany, where it is usually accompanied by a bottle of cider. The people of Brittany serve this kind of crêpe with all kinds of different fillings: *gratin dauphinois*, sausage, onions, blue cheese and so on.

---

4 servings

FOR THE CRÊPES

250 g/9 oz/2$\frac{1}{2}$ cups buckwheat flour

60 g/2 oz/6$\frac{1}{2}$ tbsp plain (all-purpose) flour

2 eggs

2 pinches of salt

750 ml/1$\frac{1}{4}$ pints/3 cups milk

FOR THE FILLING

150 ml/5 fl oz cider (hard cider)

1 kg/2$\frac{1}{4}$ lb fresh mussels, well scrubbed

800 g/1$\frac{3}{4}$ lb fresh cockles, cleaned

300 ml/10 fl oz double (heavy) cream

500 g/1 lb 2 oz leeks, chopped

60 g/2 oz fresh flat-leaf parsley

100 g/3$\frac{1}{2}$ oz white crab meat, preferably freshly cooked

---

To make the crêpe batter, put the flours in a mixing bowl and make a well in the centre. Put in the eggs and salt. Pour some of the milk into the well and mix with a wooden spoon. Gradually mix in the flour, adding the remaining milk to make a smooth and liquid batter. Cover and chill for 2 hours.

For the filling, put the cider, mussels and cockles in a large saucepan, cover and cook on a strong heat for 10 minutes or until the shells open. Stir well once. Pour into a colander set in a large bowl. Set the mussels and cockles aside.

Strain the cooking liquid through a fine sieve into a clean saucepan. Add the cream and boil to reduce to a nice sauce consistency.

Blanch the leeks in boiling salted water for 45 seconds. Drain and refresh in cold water, then squeeze dry. Blanch the parsley for 1 minute; drain and refresh, then chop it.

Pick the mussels and cockles out of their shells. Add to the sauce together with the leeks, parsley and crab meat. Keep the filling warm.

In a nonstick crêpe pan or frying pan that is about 18 cm/7 inches in diameter, cook 8 crêpes. Stack them on a plate as they are made and keep them warm.

Fill the crêpes and roll them up. Serve immediately.

Bruno's notes

● To reheat the crêpes, cover the stack with microwave-safe cling film (plastic wrap) and warm in the microwave. Or moisten each one with a little water, cover with foil and warm in a moderate oven.

● This dish can be served as a starter for 8.

Scallops and Black Pudding over Mash, Parsley and Garlic Sauce

Coquilles St Jacques et Boudin Noire sur Purée, Crème d'Ail et Persil

Scallops in French bistrots are usually prepared *à la provençale* with garlic and parsley, or maybe gratinated in their shell with a cream sauce. My dissatisfaction with routine and my love of discovering new taste combinations made me look for an alternative. Because scallops are quite an expensive ingredient for a bistrot, I wanted to combine them with a fairly cheap product to produce an affordable yet substantial dish. I tried cooking the scallops until they were nicely caramelized, and then served them over mashed potatoes with black pudding, keeping the two exciting flavours of garlic and parsley to *tatille* the scallops. The result was good, and I put the dish on my menu at the Bistrot. To everybody's surprise the dish became an instant success. A classic was born!

---

4 servings

200 ml/7 fl oz chicken stock

200 ml/7 fl oz double (heavy) cream

1 large head of garlic, separated into cloves and peeled

50 g/1¾ oz fresh flat-leaf parsley

500 g/1 lb 2 oz black pudding (blood sausage), preferably a soft one

vegetable oil

12 large scallops (sea scallops), without coral

¼ lemon

salt and freshly ground pepper

mashed potatoes (page 137)

Preheat the oven to 150°C/300°F/Gas 2.

Put the chicken stock in a saucepan and bring to the boil. Stir in the cream. Pour half of the mixture into another saucepan. Simmer the mixture in one pan until reduced to a sauce consistency. Add the garlic cloves to the other pan and leave to simmer until the garlic is very soft. Pour into a blender and blend until smooth. Season with salt and pepper.

Blanch the parsley in boiling salted water for 30 seconds. Drain well and add to the reduced sauce. Pour into the clean blender and blend until smooth. Keep the two sauces warm.

Cut the black pudding into 12 pieces and put in a baking dish. Bake for 10 minutes to heat through.

Meanwhile, heat a film of oil in a frying pan, add the scallops and cook for about 2 minutes on each side to give a nice colour. Add a squeeze of lemon juice and season with salt and pepper.

Spoon a line of mashed potatoes down the centre of each warmed plate and arrange, alternately, the scallops and black pudding on top. Spoon over the parsley sauce and then the garlic sauce. Add a grinding of pepper and serve.

Pan-fried Trout on Sour Cabbage, Smoked Herring Sauce

Truite Poelée, Chou Aigre, Crème de Hareng Fumé

		4 servings
4 trout, each weighing 220–250 g/ 8–9 oz, cleaned	50 g/$1\frac{2}{3}$ oz/$3\frac{1}{2}$ tbsp butter, cut into pieces	
100 ml/$3\frac{1}{2}$ fl oz dry white wine	$\frac{1}{4}$ lemon	
500 ml/16 fl oz water	salt and pepper	
100 ml/$3\frac{1}{2}$ fl oz double (heavy) cream	sour cabbage (page 151)	
	vegetable oil	
1 smoked herring	1 tbsp chopped fresh chives	

Fillet the trout, or have your fishmonger do this for you. Do not skin the fillets. Set them aside. Thoroughly rinse the trout bones and heads under cold running water, then put them in a saucepan with the wine and water. Bring to the boil and simmer for 20 minutes, skimming off the foam from the surface.

Strain the fish stock through a colander set in a bowl and then through a fine sieve into a clean pan. Bring to the boil and boil until reduced to 200 ml/ 7 fl oz. Add the cream and stir to mix, then boil until reduced to a sauce-like consistency. Remove from the heat. Add the smoked herring, cover and leave to infuse for 5 minutes. Pass through a fine sieve into a clean pan. Bring back to the boil, then add the butter and tilt and swirl to melt the butter and mix it into the sauce. Finish with a squeeze of lemon, and season with salt and pepper. Keep warm.

Put the cabbage in a saucepan with a bit of white wine, cover and reheat gently.

Meanwhile, heat a film of oil in a nonstick frying pan. Pan fry the trout fillets, skin side first, for 2 minutes and then the other side for about 1 minute.

Spoon the cabbage in a band in the centre of each plate and top with two trout fillets, placing them on top of each other to reshape the fish. Finish the sauce with the chives and spoon around the cabbage and fish. Serve immediately.

Bruno's notes
- All this dish needs is some boiled new potatoes.
- If the sauce needs to be reheated, bring it to the boil, whisking well. It won't separate.

POULTRY AND GAME

Whole Chicken Cooked in a Hay and Salt Crust

Poulet Fermier Cuit au Foin en Croûte de Sel

What a spectacular dish this is, yet so easy to do. When you cut the top off the salt crust, everyone around the table will smell the countryside. The chicken cooked inside will be beautifully moist, with all the amazing herb aromas. Making this dish will give you a good reason to take your children to a farm to get the hay. Or you can buy it from a pet shop.

a free-range chicken, weighing
    about 1.8 kg/4 lb
olive oil
freshly ground pepper
hay
sprigs of fresh rosemary
sprigs of fresh marjoram (optional)
1 egg yolk beaten with 1 tbsp
    water
pearl barley and pumpkin 'risotto'
    (page 153), to serve

FOR THE CRUST

1 kg/$2\frac{1}{4}$ lb/7 cups plain (all-purpose)
    flour
6 egg whites
500 g/1 lb 2 oz salt

FOR THE SAUCE

100 g/$3\frac{1}{2}$ oz/7 tbsp butter
4 tbsp Worcestershire sauce
100 ml/$3\frac{1}{2}$ fl oz chicken stock or
    water
1 tsp chopped fresh lovage
$\frac{1}{2}$ lemon

4 servings

To make the crust, combine the flour, egg whites and salt in a large bowl and beat with an electric mixer at medium speed for 1 minute. Add enough water to bind to a dough. Shape into a ball.

Preheat the oven to 150°C/300°F/Gas 2.

Brush the chicken all over with olive oil and season with pepper.

On a lightly floured surface, roll out the salt dough to an oblong about

8 mm/scant $\frac{3}{8}$ inch thick. It should be more than large enough to wrap comfortably around the chicken.

Make a bed of hay and herbs on one side of the salt dough and set the chicken on top. Brush the dough around the chicken with the egg wash. Place more hay and herbs around and over the chicken, then roll it over to wrap it completely in the salt dough. Seal all joins completely with the egg wash, pressing with your fingers. Set, seam down, on a baking sheet and bake for $1\frac{1}{2}$ hours.

Remove from the oven and leave to rest for 15 minutes.

Meanwhile, make the sauce. Put the butter in a saucepan and heat until melted and turned to a hazelnut colour. Remove from the heat and stir in the Worcestershire sauce, stock or water and lovage. Add a squeeze of lemon juice. Keep warm.

In front of your guests, cut around the circumference of the salt crust and lift off the top with the hay. Then bring the chicken back into the kitchen. Lift it out of the salt crust and discard all the hay and herbs. Cut the chicken into 4 portions.

Spoon some barley and pumpkin risotto in the centre of each warmed plate and put the chicken on top. Pour the sauce over the chicken and serve.

Bruno's notes

● You can cook the chicken 2 hours before the meal. It will keep hot for $\frac{1}{2}$ hour in its salt crust, giving you time to look after other things.

● If you can't get any lovage, you can substitute celery leaves or fresh coriander (cilantro).

Spit-roast Chicken L'Odéon

Poulet Roti à la Broche, L'Odéon

For me this dish represents the very best in cooking: it is simple yet beautifully refined. The quality of the bird is of paramount importance, and love and care must be given to its preparation. The chicken is subtly flavoured with lemon, herbs and garlic, and it is cooked slowly, with frequent basting, to ensure that the flesh remains moist and that the skin becomes crisp with a beautiful rich golden colour. No garnish or rich sauce is needed to enhance the presentation.

---

4 servings

a premium quality free-range chicken, weighing about 1.5 kg/ 3 lb 5 oz

85 g/3 oz/6 tbsp butter

2 tbsp chopped fresh flat-leaf parsley

1 lemon, halved

1 sprig of fresh thyme

6 garlic cloves, crushed with the side of a knife

$\frac{1}{2}$ Maggi chicken stock (bouillon) cube

olive oil

2 tbsp water

1 tbsp soy sauce

salt and freshly ground black pepper

Cut the wing tips from the chicken and cut out the wishbone. Starting at the neck end, use your fingers to ease the skin gently away from the meat on the breast and legs. Work slowly, wiggling your fingers from side to side in under the skin. Take care not to break the skin.

Combine the butter, parsley and juice of $\frac{1}{2}$ lemon in a food processor. Process until smooth and green. Put the butter into a piping (pastry) bag without a nozzle. Push the open end of the bag under the chicken skin, pushing it in as far as possible to the legs, and pipe the butter all over the meat on the legs and breast. Remove the bag and, with your hands, stroke the skin back in place to spread out the butter evenly.

Prepare a charcoal fire or preheat a gas grill that has a rotisserie.

Put the thyme, garlic, crumbled stock cube and remaining lemon half cut into two in the body cavity. Truss the bird. Insert the rotisserie spit into the chicken and secure firmly. Brush the chicken all over with olive oil.

Put the spit in place over or in front of the heat. After about 10 minutes of cooking, spoon the fat and juices that have dripped on to the pan underneath back over the chicken. Continue spit roasting, basting the chicken with the fat and juices every 5 minutes. Total cooking time will be about 45 minutes.

When the chicken is cooked, slide it off the spit on to a carving board. Spoon all the ingredients from the cavity into a saucepan. Add 3 tablespoons of the fat and juices, the water and soy sauce. Bring to the boil, then pass through a fine sieve into a clean pan. Reheat this *jus* and check the seasoning. Carve the chicken and serve with the *jus*.

Bruno's notes

- If you can, use a French Bresse or black-legged chicken. Guinea fowl can be prepared in the same way.

- The *jus* takes only minutes to make and, although simple, will complement the bird perfectly.

- Suggested garnishes for this are roast potatoes and French beans with *persillade* (chopped parsley and a hint of garlic).

WHOLE SNAPPER BAKED WITH LIME PICKLE AND CORIANDER, *PAGE 52*

AÏOLI PROVENÇALE, *PAGE 58*

Caramelized Chicken Thighs with Garlic and Ginger

Manchon de Volaille à l'Ail et Gingembre

Being extremely busy at the Bistrot, we haven't much time to prepare the staff meals. One day I quickly mixed all these ingredients, trying to get a balance between sweet and sour, plus a bit of ginger and garlic for character, and served it to the staff. They all loved it, and we now have this dish twice a week! I love watching people licking their fingers eating this. I think it is the best compliment.

---

16 chicken thighs

salt and freshly ground pepper

vegetable oil

200 g/7 oz onions, very finely
  chopped

8 spring onions (scallions), chopped

FOR THE GLAZE

2 tbsp HP (steak) sauce

$\frac{1}{2}$ tbsp Worcestershire sauce

1 tbsp tomato ketchup

1 tsp tomato paste

1 tbsp honey

3 tbsp malt vinegar

2 tsp dark soy sauce

2 garlic cloves, finely chopped

1 tsp finely chopped fresh ginger

4 servings

Preheat the oven to 200°C/400°F/Gas 6.

Season the chicken thighs with salt and pepper. Put them in a roasting pan with a little bit of oil and bake for about 15 minutes or until they start to get a nice golden colour.

Meanwhile, mix together the ingredients for the glaze in a small bowl.

Pour the glaze over the chicken thighs and add the chopped onions. Mix well, then return to the oven. Bake for a further 10 minutes, stirring well halfway through.

Sprinkle with the spring onions and serve with roasted new potatoes and a mixed salad.

● Heat the honey in the microwave just to melt it. It will then be easy to mix with the other ingredients.   **Bruno's note**

Wild Rabbit 'Gibelotte' with Green Peppercorns

Gibelotte de Lapin Sauvage au Poivre Vert

4 servings

2 wild rabbits, prepared for
    cooking

3 tbsp vegetable oil

90 g/3 oz/6 tbsp butter

100 g/3½ oz shallots, halved if large

200 g/7 oz button or chestnut
    mushrooms, halved or quartered
    if large

200 g/7 oz celeriac (celery root),
    cut into 2 cm/¾ inch dice

2 tsp tomato paste

400 ml/14 fl oz dry (dry hard) cider

2 tbsp Worcestershire sauce

500 ml/16 fl oz veal *jus* (page 197)

2 tsp green peppercorns packed in
    brine

½ fresh or 1 dried bay leaf

2 sprigs of fresh thyme

4 garlic cloves, crushed with the
    side of a knife

3 tbsp tarragon vinegar

salt and freshly ground pepper

chopped fresh flat-leaf parsley, to
    garnish

Cut the rabbits into pieces: front legs, back legs and saddles divided in half. Heat the oil and 50 g/1¾ oz/3½ tablespoons of the butter in a heavy-based pan until it is hot and foaming. Add the rabbit pieces and colour them on all sides. Remove them from the pan and set aside.

Add the shallots, mushrooms and celeriac to the pan and cook, stirring, until golden brown. Add the tomato paste and mix well, then deglaze the pan with the cider. Bring to the boil, stirring, and boil for 2 minutes. Add the Worcestershire sauce, veal *jus,* green peppercorns, bay leaf, thyme and garlic. Return the pieces of rabbit to the pan. Cover and leave to stew for 3 hours over very low heat, stirring occasionally.

Pour the rabbit stew through a colander set in a bowl. Remove and discard the bay leaf and thyme. Put the rabbit pieces and garnish of vegetables and peppercorns into a clean pot, cover and set aside. Strain the cooking liquid through a fine sieve into a clean pan and boil to reduce to a sauce-like consistency. Add the tarragon vinegar and remaining butter and tilt the pan to melt and swirl the butter into the sauce. Check the seasoning.

Pour the sauce over the rabbit pieces and heat, covered, for a few minutes. Serve hot, sprinkled with parsley.

● Serve this with roast potatoes or soft polenta (page 157).   **Bruno's note**

Roast Leg of Rabbit on Lime Pickle and New Potatoes with Almonds

Cuisse de Lapin Rotie, Pommes Nouvelles, Citron à l'Oriental

		4 servings
4 rabbit legs	FOR THE SAUCE	
olive oil	85 g/3 oz shallots, chopped	
150 g/5 oz onions, chopped	115 g/4 oz carrots, chopped	
85 g/3 oz sun-dried tomatoes (packed in oil), chopped	85 g/3 oz celery, chopped	
2 garlic cloves, chopped	200 g/7 oz tomatoes, preferably plum-type, seeded and chopped	
1½ tbsp chopped fresh coriander (cilantro)	100 ml/3½ fl oz white wine	
12 thin slices of pancetta	1 garlic clove, chopped	
new potatoes with almonds (page 140)	200 ml/7 fl oz veal *jus* (page 197)	
lime pickle	45 g/1½ oz/3 tbsp butter, cut into pieces	
	salt and freshly ground pepper	

Bone out the rabbit legs by cutting around the bone, but do not cut the legs open. Reserve the bones for the sauce.

In a frying pan, heat a film of olive oil and cook the onions until soft. Add the sun-dried tomatoes, the garlic and finally 1 tablespoon of the fresh coriander. Set aside on a plate until cold.

Stuff the rabbit legs with the tomato mixture. Wrap each leg in 3 slices of pancetta and tie neatly with string. Keep in the refrigerator until ready to cook.

To make the sauce, heat a little olive oil in a thick-based saucepan and add the rabbit bones. Colour them for a few minutes, then add the shallots, carrots and celery. Cook, stirring, to give the vegetables a bit of colour. Now add the chopped tomatoes, wine and garlic. Cook for a few minutes until the tomatoes are soft and pulpy. Add the veal *jus* and leave to simmer gently for 30 minutes.

Pour the sauce into a colander set in a bowl, then strain it through a fine sieve into a clean saucepan. Bring back to the boil and whisk in the butter, a few pieces at a time. Check the seasoning. Keep the sauce warm.

Heat a film of oil in the frying pan and cook the rabbit legs, covered, for about 10 minutes, turning them from time to time.

Meanwhile, toss the new potatoes with the lime pickle over a moderate heat for a minute, then add the remaining fresh coriander.

Remove the string from the rabbit legs and cut each one into 3 pieces. Put on warmed plates with the potato mixture. Pour the sauce over and serve.

Bruno's note   ● Excellent lime pickle is available in jars in many supermarkets and Indian or Pakistani shops.

Jugged Hare

Civet de Lièvre

This classic recipe is sadly neglected by restaurants, and by home cooks who probably think it takes too long and is too messy to prepare. I agree that it does require time and effort, but the dish is a treat in the autumn and winter. The gamy hare in its rich, wonderfully scented sauce is an unforgettable eating experience.

4 servings

4 hare legs

300 g/10 oz carrots

200 g/7 oz celery

250 g/9 oz onions

200 g/7 oz mushrooms, quartered if large

4 garlic cloves, crushed with the side of a knife

1 bay leaf

a few fresh sage leaves, cut if large

1 litre/1⅔ pints/1 quart red wine

vegetable oil

1 tbsp brandy

½ tbsp flour

300 ml/10 fl oz veal *jus* (page 197)

salt and pepper

blood from the hare

FOR THE GARNISH

300 g/10 oz button (pearl) onions

1 tsp sugar

1 tbsp wine vinegar

20 g/⅔ oz/4 tsp butter

120 g/4 oz streaky bacon (thick bacon slices), cut across into *lardons*

½ tbsp duck fat or vegetable oil

150 g/5 oz small button mushrooms

Put the hare legs in a large bowl. Cut the carrots, celery and onions into 2 cm/¾ inch dice and add to the bowl together with the mushrooms, garlic, bay leaf and sage. Pour in the red wine. Cover and leave to marinate in the refrigerator for 24 hours.

Drain the hare legs in a colander set in a bowl. Remove the hare legs and pat dry with paper towels. Reserve the vegetables and herbs and the marinating liquid.

Heat a film of oil in a heavy pan and sear the hare legs on all sides; remove and set aside. Put the marinade vegetables and herbs in the pan, mix well and leave to colour a bit. Return the hare legs to the pan. Pour in the brandy and set it alight. When the flames have died down, add the flour and stir well to mix. Pour in the marinating liquid and veal *jus*. Season with salt and pepper. Bring to the boil, then cover, reduce the heat and leave to simmer very gently for 3 hours or until the hare is very tender. Test by pressing it gently: it should come away from the bones.

Remove the pan from the heat and leave the hare to cool for 15–20 minutes, then carefully lift out the hare legs and set aside on a plate. Strain the sauce through a colander set in a bowl, then through a fine sieve into a clean pan. Boil the sauce until reduced to a nice consistency. Return the hare legs to the sauce, cover and set aside.

To make the garnish, combine the onions, sugar, vinegar and butter in a saucepan and add 2 pinches of salt. Pour in enough water to come level with the onions. Cover and cook until the onions are soft and tender, then uncover and boil to evaporate the liquid, stirring occasionally so the onions are glazed and coloured evenly. Set aside.

Sauté the *lardons* in the duck fat or oil. Remove with a slotted spoon and set aside. Fry the button mushrooms in the fat remaining in the pan. Set aside.

Reheat the hare legs and sauce, then stir in the *lardons,* onions and mushrooms. In a small bowl, mix a ladle of the hot sauce into the blood, then pour this into the pan, stirring well. From this point do not allow the sauce to boil or it will curdle. Cook very gently for 2–3 minutes or until the sauce thickens a bit. Check the sauce for seasoning – it should be quite peppery – and then serve.

Bruno's notes
- If the hare's blood is not available, you can use 60 g/2 oz chicken livers instead. Put them in a food processor with $3\frac{1}{2}$ tbsp red wine and blend until smooth. Press through a fine sieve, then add to the sauce. (Do not let the sauce boil once the livers have been added.)
- Suggested garnishes: *gratin dauphinois* (page 135) or creamed cauliflower with spring onions (page 145), or simply some tagliatelle pasta.

Roast Wild Duck with Elderberry Sauce

Canard Sauvage Roti au Sureau

4 wild ducks, each weighing about
  700 g/1½ lb

vegetable oil

200 g/7 oz parsnips, chopped

120 g/4 oz shallots, chopped

1 bay leaf

3 garlic cloves, crushed with the
  side of a knife

1 strip of orange zest

2 tbsp dark treacle or molasses

500 ml/16 fl oz red wine

2 tbsp red wine vinegar

200 ml/7 fl oz veal *jus* (page 197)

50 g/scant 2 oz/3½ tbsp butter

salt and pepper

2 tbsp elderberry liqueur (page 212)

4 servings

Using a heavy knife or cleaver, cut the backbone with the legs from each duck. Leave the breasts on their bone and set them aside. Cut the backbones and legs into small pieces.

Heat a film of oil in a large heavy pan and cook the chopped backbones and legs gently until coloured, stirring occasionally. Add the parsnips, shallots, bay leaf, garlic and orange zest and mix well. Cover the pan and leave to cook for about 10 minutes to soften the vegetables. Remove the lid and stir in the treacle, wine and vingegar. Bring to the boil and boil to reduce by half.

Add the veal *jus*. There should be enough liquid to come 3 cm/1¼ inches above the bones and vegetables, so add a little water if necessary. Leave to cook for 2 hours.

Preheat the oven to 200°C/400°F/Gas 6.

Strain the stock through a colander set in a bowl, then through a fine sieve into a clean pan. Boil to reduce to a sauce consistency. Pass through a fine sieve into a clean pan and set aside.

Heat a film of oil in a roasting pan on top of the stove and seal the duck breasts on all sides. Turn the breasts on to the bone side and place the pan in the oven. Cook for about 8 minutes. Remove from the oven and leave to rest in a warm place for 5 minutes.

Meanwhile, reheat the sauce to boiling. Add the butter and swirl it into the sauce. Season with salt and pepper and add the elderberry liqueur.

Take the breasts off the bone and discard the skin. Cut each breast in half and arrange on hot plates. Spoon the sauce over and serve.

Bruno's notes
- For the best flavour and most tender meat, the duck breasts should be cooked only briefly so they are still rare or medium rare, according to your taste, but no more.
- Creamed cauliflower with spring onions (page 145) is good with the dish, as are simple roast parsnips.

Roast Gressingham Duck with Olives and Cumin

Caneton de Gressingham aux Olives et Cumin

4 servings

200 g/7oz carrots
200 g/7 oz onions
100 g/3½ oz celery
2 Gressingham ducks, each
    weighing about 1–1.2 kg/
    1 lb 2 oz–2 lb 10 oz
vegetable oil or duck fat
200 g/7 oz chicken wings
5 tbsp honey
2 tbsp red wine vinegar
1 tbsp Worcestershire sauce

1 dried bay leaf
1 sprig of fresh thyme
2 garlic cloves, crushed with the
    side of a knife
1 litre/1⅔ pints/1 quart water
1 tbsp cumin seeds, freshly ground
    in a spice mill or coffee grinder
100 g/3½ oz black olives, preferably
    Niçoise, pitted
100 g/3½ oz green olives, pitted
2 tbsp extra virgin olive

Cut the carrots, onions and celery into 2 cm/$\frac{3}{4}$ inch cubes. Cut the wings off each duck (and the necks too if they are there) and reserve; set the ducks aside. Heat 3 tablespoons of vegetable oil or duck fat in a heavy saucepan, add the duck wings (and necks) and the chicken wings and cook briskly to give them a nice brown colour all over. Add the cubed vegetables and stir well, then let them get nicely coloured too. Stir in 3 tablespoons of the honey, the vinegar and Worcestershire sauce. Add the bay leaf, thyme and garlic. Pour in the water and bring to the boil. Leave to simmer for 1 hour.

Strain the stock through a colander set in a bowl and then through a fine sieve into a clean saucepan. Boil to reduce to one-third of the initial volume. Add a pinch of the freshly ground cumin to this *jus* and set aside.

Preheat the oven to 220°C/425°F/Gas 7.

Heat a film of vegetable oil in a heavy roasting pan or frying pan on top of the stove, then add the ducks and seal on all sides, turning them with two spoons. Turn the ducks on their backs and place the pan in the oven. Roast for 20–25 minutes. To check if the ducks are cooked, pull the leg away from the body and cut through the meat down to the joint: the meat at the bone should be pink but not bloody and the rest should be pinky-beige.

Remove the ducks from the oven. Turn them on to their breasts, cover with foil and leave to rest for at least 5 minutes.

Cut the legs off the ducks. Cut the breasts off the carcasses. Heat the remaining freshly ground cumin in a large frying pan over a moderate heat. When you can smell the spicy aroma, stir in the remaining honey and heat until it is warm and sticky. Add the pieces of duck, skin side down, and glaze them with the honey mixture.

Meanwhile, add the olives to the *jus* and bring to the boil. Stir in the olive oil.

Put a breast and leg of duck on each plate and spoon the olives and *jus* around. Serve immediately.

● Gressingham ducks are small (each will serve 2), but the breasts are very meaty. If you cannot get Gressingham ducks, use ducklings of another breed.   **Bruno's notes**

- When glazing the pieces of duck, take care as the honey can burn very quickly.

- I suggest you serve this with smooth broccoli purée (page 141) and roast potatoes.

Duck Confit 'au Poivre', Red Onion Marmelade

Confit de Canard au Poivre, Marmelade d'Oignon Rouge

Both duck and pork confit are an important part of the gastronomy of the South-west.

---

5 servings

5 duck legs

1 large garlic clove, chopped

1 tbsp coarse sea salt

1 tsp freshly ground black pepper

$\frac{1}{2}$ fresh or 1 dried bay leaf, snipped
   with scissors or crumbled

leaves from a few sprigs of fresh
   thyme

850 g/scant 2 lb duck fat

100 g/$3\frac{1}{2}$ oz/$\frac{1}{3}$ cup clear honey

100 ml/$3\frac{1}{2}$ fl oz red wine vinegar

2 tbsp crushed Sichuan pepper

FOR THE ONION MARMELADE

1 kg/$2\frac{1}{4}$ lb red onions

4 tbsp duck fat

200 ml/7 fl oz red wine vinegar

The day before, place the duck legs on a tray, flesh side up. Rub with the chopped garlic, then sprinkle over the salt, pepper, bay leaf and thyme. Cover tightly and set aside in the refrigerator for at least 8 hours. After this time, the flesh should have absorbed the salt and all the other flavours.

Rinse the duck legs under cold running water, then put them in a large saucepan with the duck fat. Simmer for about 2 hours. Check if the duck is cooked by pricking with a skewer – if the skewer gets through with only a slight resistance and pulls out easily without pulling the leg, the confit is cooked. Leave to cool in the fat.

To make the onion marmelade, cut the onions in half, then cut out the hard piece at the base. Slice the onions finely. In a thick-based pan heat the duck fat and add the onions. Cover with a lid and cook very slowly to melt and caramelize the onions. This will take about 1 hour. After 45 minutes of cooking, add the vinegar.

When ready to serve, preheat the grill (broiler) to moderate.

Put the honey and vinegar in a small pan and boil to reduce to a sticky consistency.

Scrape all the fat from the duck legs and arrange them on a baking tray. Spoon the honey mixture over the duck and sprinkle with the Sichuan pepper. Place under the grill and cook for 5 minutes, then turn up the heat to full and continue cooking until the top becomes crisp and nicely coloured.

Spoon the hot onion marmalade on the centre of each plate and set the duck confit on top.

- During the cooking of the confit, add about 150 ml / 5 fl oz of water every $\frac{1}{2}$ hour to prevent the fat burning and to give moisture to the duck.
- My mother used to say that confit is cooked when a blown straw from a broom can get through without difficulty.
- You can keep the garlic and herbs and use them to flavour sauces.
- It's worth preparing confit in large quantities, because it will be a great help when you have unexpected guests. For 10 duck legs, double the flavourings and use enough duck fat to cover the legs. You can keep the cooled confit, covered with fat, in the refrigerator or another cool place for up to 2 weeks.

Bruno's notes

Wood Pigeon with Garlic, Onions and Penne

Pigeon des Bois Roti à l'Ail, Penne

---

4 servings

6 wood (squab) pigeons

24 button (pearl) onions, peeled

24 garlic cloves, peeled

80 g/scant 3 oz/$5\frac{1}{2}$ tbsp butter

1 tsp sugar

2 tbsp red wine vinegar

2 tbsp water

200 g/7 oz penne

olive oil

1 tbsp chopped fresh flat-leaf
  parsley

FOR THE SAUCE

vegetable oil

150 g/5 oz onions, chopped

150 g/5 oz parsnips, chopped

100 g/$3\frac{1}{2}$ oz celeriac (celery root),
  chopped

100 ml/$3\frac{1}{2}$ fl oz red wine vinegar

2 tbsp honey

$\frac{1}{2}$ fresh or 1 dried bay leaf

500 ml/16 fl oz chicken stock

1 tbsp dark soy sauce

1 tbsp Worcestershire sauce

50 g/$1\frac{3}{4}$ oz/$3\frac{1}{2}$ tbsp butter, cut into
  pieces

salt and freshly ground pepper

Preheat the oven to 180°C/350°F/Gas 4.

   With a sharp knife, cut the boneless breasts from the pigeons, keeping each breast in a neat piece and leaving on the skin. Set the 12 breasts aside. Chop up the pigeon carcasses and legs, using a heavy knife.

   To make the sauce, heat a film of vegetable oil in a large, heavy-based saucepan and fry the pigeon bones until lightly browned. Remove them and reserve. Add the chopped onions, parsnips and celeriac to the pan and cook until nicely coloured. Return the bones to the pan and add the vinegar, honey and bay leaf. Boil until the liquid has evaporated and the ingredients are sticky and caramelized. Add the chicken stock, soy sauce and Worcestershire sauce. Bring to the boil, then leave to simmer for about 1 hour.

Meanwhile, press a doubled sheet of foil into a soup plate (to mould it). Put the button onions and garlic cloves in the centre of the foil and add 50 g/ 1¾ oz/3½ tablespoons of the butter, the sugar, vinegar and water. Wrap up the foil into a tight parcel. Set the foil parcel on a baking sheet and cook in the oven for 45 minutes.

Pour the sauce into a colander set in a bowl, then strain the resulting liquid through a fine sieve into a clean saucepan. Bring to the boil and boil until reduced to a sauce-like consistency, skimming occasionally to remove any impurities that rise to the surface. Add the butter and tilt the pan to melt and swirl the butter into the sauce. Check the seasoning. Keep the sauce warm.

Cook the pasta in a large pan of boiling salted water until it is al dente (check the packet directions for timing). Drain and refresh in cold water.

Heat a film of olive oil in a frying pan and cook the pigeon breasts briskly for 2 minutes on each side. Remove them to a plate, cover and set aside in a warm place.

Melt the remaining butter in the frying pan and add the pasta and the button onions and garlic with their juices. Toss together over the heat until hot. Stir in the parsley.

Cut each pigeon breast into 4 and arrange on hot plates. Cover with the pasta mixture and spoon the sauce over.

Bruno's notes

● A final touch of a few drops of walnut oil on each serving will give an interesting 'woodsy' flavour to the dish.

● If after cooking in the oven, the button onions and garlic do not have enough colour, tip them from the foil into the frying pan, with all their juices, and fry over a high heat until golden brown. Then add the pasta and butter.

● You can use celeriac peelings and trimmings.

● If, by chance, you can get fresh cèpes, sauté them with the button onion mixture.

Pheasant 'Crépinette' with Gingered Pear

Crépinette de Faisan Roti, Poire au Gingembre

In France pheasant is an expensive treat, but in England pheasant is quite common and cheap. In fact, in season pheasant is cheaper than a free-range chicken! It is difficult to cook pheasant on the bone without the meat becoming dry, so in this recipe I have boned the birds. This makes the cooking easy to control, and the dish much easier to eat.

4 servings

2 young pheasants, preferably hens

200 g/7 oz streaky bacon (thick bacon slices)

80 g/scant 3 oz chicken livers

salt and freshly ground pepper

pork caul

vegetable oil

80 g/scant 3 oz shallots, chopped

150 g/5 oz carrots, chopped

150 g/5 oz parsnips, chopped

100 g/3½ oz celery, chopped

1 garlic clove, crushed with the side of a knife

1 dried bay leaf

100 ml/3½ fl oz white wine

600 ml/1 pint/2½ cups chicken stock

1 tbsp soy sauce

FOR THE GINGERED PEARS

100 g/3½ oz honey

100 ml/3½ fl oz red wine vinegar

1 tsp finely chopped fresh ginger

2 firm dessert pears, peeled, halved and cored

Cut the pheasant legs and breasts off the carcasses. Set the breasts aside. Cut the drumsticks from the thighs. Remove the bones from the thighs. Set the carcasses, drumsticks and thigh bones aside. Finely chop the meat from the thighs with the bacon and livers. Season this *farce* with salt and pepper.

Lay the breasts on the work surface, skin side down. Season with salt and pepper. Spread the *farce* over the breasts. Roll each breast in a piece of caul. Arrange on a plate, cover and refrigerate until ready to cook.

Coarsely chop the pheasant carcasses. Heat 4 tablespoons of vegetable oil in a heavy saucepan and add the carcasses, drumsticks and thigh bones. Cook briskly, stirring, until well coloured. Remove all the bones from the pan with a slotted spoon and reserve them. Add the chopped vegetables with the garlic and bay leaf. Mix well, then cook until the vegetables are nicely golden. Deglaze the pan with the white wine and bring to the boil. Return the bones. Add the chicken stock and soy sauce and bring back to the boil. Leave to simmer for 1 hour.

Meanwhile, prepare the gingered pears. Combine the honey, vinegar and ginger in a heavy saucepan and boil to reduce to a thick consistency; the syrup will turn to golden brown. Add the pears and toss to glaze them. Add 4 tablespoons of the pheasant stock. Cover and leave to cook very gently for 15 minutes or until the pears are tender. Set aside.

When the stock has finished cooking, strain it through a colander set in a bowl, then through a fine sieve into a clean pan. Boil to reduce to a sauce-like consistency. Set aside.

Heat a film of oil in a frying pan over moderate heat. Put the pheasant *crépinettes* in the pan, flesh side down. Cover the pan and leave to cook for 8 minutes. Turn the crépinettes over and cook, covered, for about 6 minutes longer.

Just before serving, reheat the pears and cook uncovered to reduce and glaze them. Reheat the sauce if necessary.

On each plate place a pheasant *crépinette*, cut into three, and a gingered pear half. Spoon the sauce around and serve.

Bruno's notes

- Be careful when you buy pheasant – some birds, particularly frozen ones, are so lean that after cooking their meat is like a tasteless piece of leather. Ideally pheasants should have a thin layer of yellow fat under the skin. You will have to rely on your butcher to give you good advice.
- The best pears to use for this are William's or Bartlett, Packham and Conference.
- I suggest you serve this with spinach with almonds and nutmeg (page 142).

Boudin Blanc with Onion Gravy

Boudin Blanc Sauce à l'Oignon

In France it is still possible to find good quality *boudin blanc* in charcuteries, even though the real charcutiers are disappearing to be replaced by machines in factories. In the big foodstores like Casino, especially around Christmas, *boudin blanc* is easily obtainable. But in Britain, only a few specialized butchers are able to supply *boudin blanc* from time to time, so I started to make my own. I think mine are more flavourful than the commercial ones, with a strong seasoning of nutmeg to counteract the richness, and they are lighter in texture. Cream sauce with wild mushrooms is the classic partner for *boudin blanc*, but I like to serve them with a sweet onion gravy.

4 servings

300 ml/10 fl oz milk

½ fresh or 1 dried bay leaf

100 g/3½ oz onions, very thinly sliced

3 slices of white bread

2 skinless boneless chicken breasts (breast halves)

100 g/3½ oz *foie gras*

4 pinches of grated nutmeg

salt and freshly ground pepper

3 eggs, at room temperature

300 ml/10 fl oz double (heavy) cream

1 metre/3 feet 3 inches of sausage casing

vegetable oil

30 g/1 oz/2 tbsp butter

pearl barley and pumpkin 'risotto' (page 153)

1 tbsp chopped fresh chives

FOR THE ONION GRAVY

1 tbsp duck fat or butter

350 g/12 oz onions, cut into 1.5 cm/½ inch cubes

2 garlic cloves, chopped

1 sprig of fresh thyme

100 ml/3½ fl oz white wine

300 ml/10 fl oz veal *jus* (page 197) or poultry *jus* (page 195)

150 ml/5 fl oz water

Put the milk in a saucepan with the bay leaf and onions. Bring to the boil and simmer for about 30 minutes or until the milk has almost all evaporated and only 3 tablespoons remain. Remove from the heat and add the white bread. Mix with a wooden spoon until the bread has absorbed all the liquid and a paste is formed. This is called a *panade*.

Combine the chicken breasts and *panade* in a food processor. Process for 2 minutes, then add the *foie gras*, nutmeg, salt and pepper. Process again until very smooth. Add the eggs, one at a time, mixing well. Finally, mix in the cream. Pass this *farce* through a fine sieve set in a bowl. Leave to rest in the refrigerator for 30 minutes.

Meanwhile, make the onion gravy. Heat the duck fat or butter in a frying pan, add the onions and cook until soft and golden. Add the garlic, thyme and white wine and mix well. Bring to the boil and boil for 1 minute, then add the veal *jus* and water. Leave to cook gently for 30 minutes, stirring occasionally. At the end of cooking, season with salt and pepper and set aside.

While the onion gravy is cooking, pipe the *farce* into the sausage casing, without packing it too tightly. Tie the two ends. Bring a large pan of water to simmering point. Add the *boudin blanc* and cook gently for 10 minutes. Be sure the water remains just below a simmer. Remove from the heat, cover and leave for 15 minutes.

Drain the *boudin blanc* and plunge into iced water. When the *boudin* are cool enough to handle, carefully remove the skin. Heat a film of oil in a frying pan and colour the *boudin blanc* lightly on all sides over a gentle heat. Add the butter, then turn the heat to very low, cover the pan and leave to cook for a few minutes to heat through.

Spoon the barley and pumpkin risotto in the centre of each plate and set the *boudin blanc* on top. Spoon the onion gravy over the *boudin blanc* and sprinkle with chives. Serve immediately.

● If you don't have sausage casing, you can use cling film (plastic wrap). Stretch it **Bruno's note** tightly when rolling up, twist the ends and tie over the top of each *boudin* into a knot.

Grilled Quails with Salsify, Brown Butter with Nuts and Sultanas

Caille Grillé au Salsifis, Beurre Noisette et Raisins Secs

---

4 servings

1 lemon, halved

800 g/1¾ lb salsify

50 g/1¾ oz/⅓ cup plain (all-purpose) flour dissolved in a glass of water

8 quails

salt and freshly ground black pepper

olive oil

2 tbsp water

180 g/6 oz/¾ cup butter

1 tbsp flaked (sliced) almonds

½ tbsp skinned pistachios, slightly crushed with the side of a knife

½ tbsp pine kernels (nuts)

4 tbsp balsamic vinegar

2 tbsp sultanas (golden raisins), soaked in warm water for 3 hours and drained

1 tbsp chopped fresh flat-leaf parsley

Squeeze the juice of ½ lemon into a bowl of water. Peel the salsify and drop them immediately into the water to prevent them discolouring. When all are peeled, cut them into pieces about 6 cm/2½ inches long.

Bring a pan of salted water to the boil. Add the remaining lemon juice and the flour mixture. Whisk well, then add the salsify. Simmer for about 15 minutes. Remove from the heat and set aside, leaving the salsify in the liquid.

Preheat a ridged cast iron grill pan, or prepare a charcoal fire. Preheat the oven to 220°C/425°F/Gas 7.

Season the quails with salt and pepper and brush all over with olive oil. Lay them on the hot pan, or on the grill over the charcoal, and grill to colour on all sides. Transfer the quails to an oiled roasting pan and finish cooking in the oven, 5–10 minutes.

Drain and rinse the salsify. Put it in a small pan with the water and a nut of butter. Heat, tossing to coat the pieces of salsify, then cover the pan and leave to warm through for a few minutes on a very low heat.

Meanwhile, melt the remaining butter in a small frying pan and add the nuts. Heat until the butter turns light brown (*noisette*). At this exact point, remove from the heat and stir in the vinegar and sultanas. Season with salt and pepper.

Spoon the salsify in the centre of the plates and put the quails on top. Stir the parsley into the sauce, then spoon it over the quails and salsify. Serve immediately.

● Leaving the salsify in its cooking liquid (which is called a *blanc*) prevents it from discolouring. **Bruno's note**

Cassoulet du Sud Ouest

In France, cassoulet is the second best-selling ready-meal in a can, very close to ravioli, which comes in first position. Cassoulet is also the most common bistrot dish. You can find very good canned cassoulet in France, but the best is the one you make at home, cooked very slowly in the oven and finished with a beautiful gratinated breadcrumb top. When you make cassoulet you have to prepare it in large quantities, so it is the ideal dish for a large party, easy to reheat in the oven and with no last-minute preparation.

I was brought up on cassoulet. It is a dish originally from Languedoc, although many people dispute this and will tell you that it was created in Castelnaudary near Toulouse. When you go further south, near Carcassonne, lamb is added to cassoulet. In the South-west we normally make it with duck confit, pork knuckles and sausages.

Like other hotpots, cassoulet is a dish of generosity. I hope you enjoy this marvel of French regional gastronomy.

10 servings

500 g/1 lb 2 oz carrots

500 g/1 lb 2 oz onions

300 g/10 oz celery

2 tbsp duck fat, from the confit

5 garlic cloves, chopped

1 bunch of fresh thyme

$\frac{1}{2}$ fresh or 1 dried bay leaf

2 tbsp tomato paste

800 g–1 kg/1$\frac{3}{4}$–2$\frac{1}{4}$ lb dried white beans, soaked overnight and drained

250 ml/8 fl oz white wine

3 salted pork knuckles (salted ham hocks)

salt and freshly ground pepper

10 Toulouse sausages or other good-quality seasoned fresh pork sausages

5 legs of duck confit (page 92), fat scraped off and each leg cut into 2 pieces

200 g/7 oz/4$\frac{1}{2}$ cups fresh breadcrumbs

Preheat the oven to 120°C/245°F/Gas $\frac{1}{4}$. Cut the carrots, onions and celery into 1.5 cm/$\frac{1}{2}$ inch cubes. In a large pot (Le Creuset type) put the duck fat to melt. When the fat is hot, add the prepared vegetables and mix with a wooden spoon. Cook for 2 minutes without colouring them.

Add the garlic, thyme, bay leaf, tomato paste and the beans. Pour in the white wine and bring to the boil. Simmer for 3 minutes, then add the pork knuckles. Add enough cold water to cover the ingredients and bring to simmering point.

Put the lid on the pot and transfer to the oven. Cook for 2 hours.

Season the beans. Add the sausages, pushing them down into the mixture. Cook, covered, for 15 minutes, then add the duck confit and cook for another 15 minutes.

Check the seasoning. Sprinkle the breadcrumbs over the top of the cassoulet. Cook in the oven, uncovered, for a final 30 minutes.

To serve, just put the pot in the middle of the table.

Bruno's notes

- Use white haricot beans, or navy beans in the US.
- For a richer flavour, just scrape the fat off the duck. Otherwise, steam or microwave to melt the fat and pour it off.

Meat

Due to a current preoccupation with healthy eating, red meat, offal and game seem to have been banned from our diet, and now chicken, turkey, white fish and pasta are on the front line! Well, I have to say that I do not agree with the trends. I believe in diversity. If your diet is varied, and includes greens, dried beans and peas, fresh vegetables, fruits, meats and so on – with less beer and, of course, more red wine – I think you will have a much more enjoyable and healthy life. Everything is good in reasonable quantities.

Grilled Steak with Herb Butter

Steak Frites, Beurre Maître d'Hôtel

---

4 servings

4 pieces of sirloin steak, beef skirt
   or beef flank, each weighing
   200–250 g/7–9 oz
2 tbsp vegetable oil
salt and freshly ground black
   pepper
butter
frites (page 139) to serve

FOR THE BEURRE MAÎTRE D'HÔTEL
80 g/scant 3 oz/6 tbsp butter at
   room temperature, cubed
1 tsp very finely chopped shallot
1 tbsp finely chopped parsley
1 tsp finely chopped fresh chives
$\frac{1}{2}$ tsp finely chopped fresh tarragon
$\frac{1}{2}$ tsp Dijon mustard
juice of $\frac{1}{4}$ lemon

Two hours before serving, prepare the *beurre maître d'hôtel*. Put the butter in a small bowl and add the remaining ingredients. Mix very well together with a fork and season to taste with salt and pepper. Spoon the herb butter on to the centre of a piece of foil and roll up tightly into a neat sausage shape. Twist the ends of the foil to seal. Refrigerate to set the butter.

    Preheat the oven to 220°C/425°F/Gas 7. Heat a ridged cast iron grill pan (this will take about 10 minutes). At the same time, brush the steaks with a little oil.

    Lay the steaks on the hot grill pan. After about 30 seconds, give each steak a quarter-turn so that it will be scored with a criss-cross pattern. After another 30 seconds, turn the steaks over and repeat the procedure on the other side. Transfer the steaks to an oven tray. Season with salt and freshly ground black pepper and top each with a small piece of butter. Finish cooking in the hot oven to your taste – about 3 minutes for rare and 4–5 minutes for medium.

Put a slice or two of herb butter on each steak and serve immediately, with frites.

Bruno's notes

- It is important to season the meat *after* grilling because doing it before cooking will draw out the juices.
- Take the herb butter out the refrigerator about 5 minutes before slicing it.
- The choice of the right steak for grilling is vital. A slice from the rump is my favourite because I think the flavour is more developed. It is also a good piece for a *steak au poivre*. Skirt is very juicy, although its stringy texture puts off the burger lovers (what a shame!). Flank is not as easy to find – perhaps because it is enjoyed by the butchers themselves. Sirloin is good as long as it is well marbled with fat, although the flavour is sometimes disappointing. For the inexperienced shopper sirloin is probably the safest choice.

Pot-au-Feu

Pot-au-feu is probably the most famous French dish in the world. It should contain at least two kinds of meat, a lean 'muscle' cut and a fatty one.

Cabbage is added in some parts of France. I like a stuffed cabbage in my pot-au-feu because it gives a lot of flavour and looks very homely.

8 servings

800 g/1¾ lb beef flat (short) ribs

800 g/1¾ lb shin of beef on the bone (shank cross-cuts)

8 pork spare ribs

1 small boiling fowl (stewing chicken)

coarse sea salt

400 g/14 oz carrots

300 g/10 oz leeks

300 g/10 oz turnips

200 g/7 oz celery

300 g/10 oz swede (rutabaga)

250 g/9 oz onions

4 garlic cloves, crushed with the side of a knife

1 bay leaf

1 sprig of fresh thyme

2 cloves

8 black peppercorns

FOR THE STUFFED CABBAGE

1 large Savoy cabbage

500 g/1 lb 2 oz minced (ground) pork

100 g/3½ oz chicken livers, trimmed and chopped

4 slices of white bread, moistened with milk

2 eggs

1 tbsp chopped fresh flat-leaf parsley

salt and freshly ground pepper

TO SERVE

Dijon mustard

salsa verde (page 199)

coarse salt

Put the beef flat ribs and shin in a large pot with the spare ribs and boiling fowl. Cover with enough water to come 10 cm/4 inches above the meats. Add 1 tablespoon of sea salt. Bring to the boil, skimming off the foam.

Cut all the vegetables into large pieces and add to the pot. Add the garlic, herbs, cloves and peppercorns. Leave to simmer while you prepare the cabbage.

Working from the base, cut the core out of the cabbage. Separate the leaves. Blanch the leaves in a large pan of boiling salted water for 1 minute, then drain and refresh. Pat dry with a clean cloth.

Mix together the pork, chicken livers, bread, eggs and parsley. Add some salt and pepper. Starting with the yellow leaves from the heart of the cabbage, put a bit of the pork *farce* on each leaf and reshape the cabbage, overlapping the leaves as you go. Wrap the reshaped cabbage in a piece of muslin or cheesecloth or a clean kitchen cloth and tie firmly at the top with string.

Plunge the cabbage into the pot-au-feu. Cover the pot and leave to simmer for about 2 hours.

Lift the cabbage out of the pot and unwrap it. Cut it into 8 wedges. With a slotted spoon, remove the meat and vegetables from the pot. Cut into serving pieces and arrange on a large platter with the cabbage wedges, vegetables on one side and meat on the other. Serve with Dijon mustard, coarse sea salt and a sauceboat of salsa verde.

Bruno's notes

● When bringing the liquid to the boil at the beginning of the cooking, it is important to skim off all the impurities that rise to the surface.

● I often add 1 or 2 tablespoons of dark soy sauce with the vegetables for a more richly coloured bouillon.

● Traditionally, the bouillon is strained and served separately as a soup.

● Leftover pot-au-feu makes a great salad. Try it with the balsamic vinegar dressing on page 207.

● The bouillon can be boiled with a calf's foot until reduced and then strained and set in a mould with any leftover meat and vegetables cut into dice. Slice it to serve with mayonnaise.

Rich Beef Stew

Daube de Boeuf à l'Ancienne

Who could fail to be entranced by the aroma of a *daube* simmering on the stove? This stew is number one in the list of *plat mijoté*, or simmered dishes, which are so much a part of the French culinary tradition. I have always loved stews like this. When I started working at Gastronome One 13

years ago, *daubes* featured prominently on my menus. This was a natural choice for me, having been brought up in the tradition of *cuisine du terroir*. Today, especially in autumn and winter, I enjoy a nice *daube* with mashed potatoes and, no doubt, I still will in 20 years' time.

---

4 servings

300 g/10 oz onions

300 g/10 oz carrots

200 g/7 oz celery

vegetable oil

1.2 kg/2 lb 10 oz ox cheek (with skin), cut into 6 cm/2½ inch cubes

1 bay leaf

1 sprig of fresh thyme

3 garlic cloves, crushed with the side of a knife

750 ml/1¼ pints/3 cups full-bodied red wine, such as North African

1 litre/1⅔ pints/1 quart canned beef consommé

30 g/1 oz/2 tbsp soft butter

30 g/1 oz/3 tbsp flour

salt and freshly ground black pepper

FOR THE GARNISH

200 g/7 oz button (pearl) onions

2 tsp sugar

30 g/1 oz/2 tbsp butter

150 g/5 oz streaky bacon (thick bacon slices), cut across into *lardons*

150 g/5 oz button mushrooms

300 g/10 oz carrots, sliced

Roughly chop the onions, carrots and celery and set aside. Heat a film of oil in a large heavy-based pan or flameproof casserole. Add the cubes of meat, a few at a time, and brown all over over a brisk heat. Remove the meat and set aside. Put the carrots, onions, celery, bay leaf, thyme and garlic in the pan and mix well. Cook for about 15 minutes to brown nicely, stirring occasionally.

Add the wine and stir well. Bring to the boil and simmer for 3 minutes, then add the consommé. Return the meat to the pan. The liquid level should be 3 cm/$1\frac{1}{4}$ inches above the meat and vegetables so add water if necessary. Bring back to simmering point, then cover and leave to cook over a low heat for 2 hours.

Mix the soft butter with the flour in a small bowl. Add a ladle of the liquid from the pan and mix well, then return this to the pan, stirring with a wooden spoon. Leave to cook, covered, for a further 1 hour. During this time, stir well from time to time to be sure the sauce is not sticking to the bottom of the pan.

To prepare the garnish, put the button onions in a small saucepan and just cover with salted water. Add the sugar and butter and cook until all the water has evaporated and the onions are tender and golden brown. Remove from the heat and set aside.

Heat a film of oil in a frying pan and sauté the *lardons* until they are golden brown. Remove with a slotted spoon and drain on paper towels. Add the button mushrooms to the pan and fry until they are golden brown. Remove and set aside.

Remove the pieces of meat from the sauce and reserve. Strain the sauce through a colander set in a bowl, then pass through a fine sieve into a clean pan. Reheat the sauce. Add the sliced carrots and simmer gently for about 20 minutes. Skim off any fat and foam that rises to the surface.

When the sauce has reduced to a nice consistency, add the *lardons*, button onions and mushrooms. Return the pieces of meat. Heat everything through and check the seasoning. Serve with mashed potatoes (page 137).

Bruno's notes

- The choice of meat for a *daube* is very important. My preference is ox cheek, which is very tender, moist and full of flavour. Oxtail would be my second choice, and then shin of beef (beef shank). Ask your butcher, and ask again as he probably keeps these cuts for himself! If using oxtail you'll need 2 kg/$4\frac{1}{2}$ lb; have it cut into 4 cm/$1\frac{1}{2}$ inch pieces. For shin of beef, buy 1.2 kg/2 lb 10 oz (weight without bone); cut it into cubes.

- If you use shin of beef it will take only $1\frac{1}{2}$ hours to cook.

- Ideally, a *daube* made with ox cheek or shin of beef should be made 3 days in advance. Reheat it thoroughly each day, then cool it quickly. This is an old trick to enhance the flavour.

Beef Birds in Juniper Sauce

Oiseaux sans Têtes, Sauce Genièvre

This dish has nothing to do with birds, but it is thought that the shape of the little 'packages' is like that of headless birds, which is why the dish is called *oiseaux sans têtes* in French. When I was a boy my mother tried to convince me that they were birds, but she didn't trick me – I could taste the difference.

4 servings

4 thin slices of beef skirt, each weighing about 150 g/5 oz

duck fat or vegetable oil

120 g/4 oz shallots, chopped

250 g/9 oz carrots, cut into 5 mm/¼ inch dice

2 celery stalks, diced

20 juniper berries, coarsely crushed

1 garlic clove, finely chopped

2 tsp tomato paste

300 ml/10 fl oz chicken stock

1 sprig of fresh thyme

1 bay leaf

1 tbsp chopped blanched flat-leaf parsley

50 g/1¾ oz/3½ tbsp butter, cut into small pieces

FOR THE STUFFING

200 g/7 oz streaky bacon (thick bacon slices), chopped

3 slices of white bread, moistened with 4 tbsp milk

1 egg

2 garlic cloves, chopped

1 tbsp chopped fresh flat-leaf parsley

salt and freshly ground pepper

vegetable oil

200 g/7 oz mushrooms, sliced

To make the stuffing, combine the bacon, bread, egg, garlic, parsley and some salt and pepper in a food processor and process to a coarse-textured mixture. Heat a film of oil in a frying pan and sauté the mushrooms until they are just wilted. Add to the stuffing mixture.

Lay the slices of beef flat on the work surface and season them with salt and pepper. Divide the stuffing equally among the slices, then roll them up, tucking in the sides. Tie a piece of string lengthwise around each 'bird', then tie crosswise in two or three places.

Heat a spoonful of duck fat or a film of oil in a heavy-based saucepan. Add the beef birds and seal on all sides. Add the shallots, carrots, celery, juniper berries and garlic and mix well. Cook for 5 minutes, then stir in the tomato paste. Cook for a further 3 minutes. Add the stock, thyme and bay leaf and bring to simmering point, then cover and leave to cook gently for about 40 minutes.

Remove the beef birds and keep them warm, covered. Discard the thyme and bay leaf from the sauce, then boil until it is reduced to about 180 ml/6 fl oz. Add the parsley and butter and tilt the pan to melt and swirl the butter into the sauce. Check the seasoning.

Cut the strings from the beef birds, then place them on plates and spoon the sauce over. A smooth broccoli purée such as the one on page 141 would be a good accompaniment.

Bruno's notes

- You can substitute veal escalopes (flattened veal cutlets) or flattened boneless chicken breasts for the slices of beef.
- If you like, wrap each beef bird in a slice of Parma ham before tying.
- The chicken stock can be replaced by white wine plus $\frac{1}{4}$ Maggi chicken stock (bouillon) cube.
- Serve with peas French-style (page 143) and fondant potatoes (page 138).

Garbure Béarnaise

In autumn and winter my mother sometimes made a superb cabbage soup, full of vegetables and enriched with the top bone end of a dried ham and a bit of duck confit. This soup was a meal in itself – starter and main course all in one! The big clay pot was put in the centre of the table, and the only sound to be heard was that of my family enjoying the feast. When my father had nearly finished his second helping, he would stop and leave a few spoonfuls of the delicious bouillon in his plate. To this he added a glass of red wine and then drank it all. This is a tradition amongst farmers, called *faire chabrot*, and probably was just a reason to have a bit more wine.

4 servings

1 salted pork knuckle (salted ham hock), soaked overnight

50 g/1¾ oz/¼ cup dried butter (lima) beans, soaked overnight and drained

200 g/7 oz carrots, cut into 4 cm/1½ inch chunks

100 g/3½ oz celery, cut into 5 cm/2 inch pieces

200 g/7 oz swede (rutabaga), cut into large cubes

200 g/7 oz leeks, cut into 5 cm/2 inch pieces

3 garlic cloves, crushed with the side of a knife

1 bouquet garni (page 209)

10 black peppercorns, coarsely crushed

1 Savoy cabbage, cored and cut into 3 cm/1¼ inch squares

2 legs of duck confit (page 92), fat scraped off and each cut into 2

1 tbsp chopped fresh chives

1 tbsp chopped fresh flat-leaf parsley

TO SERVE

coarse salt

pepper mill

Put the pork knuckle in a large deep pot and pour in enough water to come 5 cm/2 inches above the knuckle. Bring to the boil, then lower the heat and skim the foam from the surface. Leave to simmer for 15 minutes, skimming off all the foam that rises.

Add the butter beans, carrots, celery, swede, leeks, garlic, bouquet garni and peppercorns. Cover and leave to simmer for 1 hour.

Add the cabbage and simmer for a further 1½ hours.

Add the duck confit and simmer for a final 10 minutes.

Lift the knuckle out of the pot. Take the meat from the bones and return it to the pot; discard the bones. Stir the chives and parsley into the bouillon. To serve, divide the meat and vegetables among soup plates and add a ladleful of bouillon. Serve with coarse sea salt and coarsely crushed black peppercorns.

Braised Veal Tendron with Pumpkin and Parmesan Purée

Tendron de Veau Braisé, Purée de Potiron au Parmesan

This recipe uses one of my favourite cuts of veal, taken from the breast. It is made up of meat, fat and soft gristle. The meat becomes wonderfully succulent after cooking in this way, and has an amazing flavour.

---

olive oil

4 veal tendrons (from the breast),
   total weight about 1 kg/2¼ lb

200 g/7 oz carrots, chopped

250 g/9 oz onions, chopped

1 can (400 g/14 oz) plum tomatoes,
   drained

3 garlic cloves, chopped

1 sprig of fresh rosemary

½ tbsp chopped fresh sage

250 ml/8 fl oz white wine

60 g/2 oz/4 tbsp butter, cut into
   pieces

salt and freshly ground pepper

pumpkin and Parmesan purée
   (page 152), to serve

1 tbsp chopped fresh chives

4 servings

Heat a film of olive oil in a large sauté pan. Add the tendrons and colour lightly on all sides. Add the carrots, onions, tomatoes, garlic, rosemary, sage and white wine. Bring to the boil and simmer for 5 minutes.

Add enough water to come level with the ingredients in the pan. Bring back to the boil, then reduce the heat so the liquid is just simmering. Cover and leave to cook for about 1½ hours.

Take the pieces of meat out of the pan and set aside, covered. Strain the cooking liquid into a clean pan. Boil until reduced to about 250 ml/8 fl oz, skimming occasionally. Add the butter and tilt the pan to melt the butter and swirl it into the sauce. Taste and add salt and pepper.

Put the veal tendrons on the plates with the pumpkin and Parmesan purée. Spoon the sauce over and sprinkle with chives.

Bruno's notes

- It is important to colour the veal tendrons slowly, to allow the sugars from the meat to caramelize. If you do this too fast, you will just dry the outside, and the flavour of the finished dish will not be as good.

- You can add some tiny capers to the sauce at the last minute. Or, if by chance you can get a black truffle, some chopped in the sauce will be a rare treat. Another idea is to add a bit of saffron and grated orange zest to the sauce with the butter.

MACKEREL KEBAB WITH PICCALILLI, *PAGE 64*

SCALLOPS AND BLACK PUDDING OVER MASH, PARSLEY AND GARLIC SAUCE, *PAGE 76*

WHOLE CHICKEN COOKED IN A HAY AND SALT CRUST, *PAGE 79*

ROAST LEG OF RABBIT ON LIME PICKLE AND NEW POTATOES WITH ALMONDS, *PAGE 85*

Irish Stew (my way)

Ragout Irlandais à ma façon

The cooking method here was inspired by the system used at the beginning of this century, when women took their baking and other oven cooking to the village baker on their way to the *lavoir*. While they washed the family linen, their dinner was cooking in the baker's oven. I applied this concept to the famous Irish Stew, which I love, and changed the water to sheep's milk. It makes a wonderful dish for cold days.

---

800 g/1¾ lb boneless lamb shoulder, trimmed

800 g/1¾ lb potatoes

600 g/1 lb 5 oz leeks, chopped

4 garlic cloves, chopped

2 litres/3½ pints/2 quarts sheep's milk

salt and freshly ground pepper

200 g/7 oz/1½ cups flour

2 tbsp chopped fresh flat-leaf parsley

4 servings

Preheat the oven to 120°C/245°F/Gas ¼.

Cut the lamb into 3 cm/1¼ inch chunks. Peel the potatoes and cut into chunks of the same size.

Combine the lamb, potatoes, leeks and garlic in a large stew pot or other heavy casserole. Pour in the sheep's milk and season with salt and pepper. Put the lid on the pot.

In a small bowl, mix the flour with enough water to make a thick paste. Use this to seal the lid on to the pot. Cook in the oven for 3 hours.

Break open the seal and serve the stew sprinkled with parsley.

● If you can't get any sheep's milk, you can use cow's milk instead.

Bruno's note

Poached Lamb Shoulder Stuffed with Haggis and Served with Horseradish Mayonnaise

Epaule d'Agneau Farcie de Haggis, Mayonnaise au Raifort

4 servings

a boned lamb shoulder weighing
about 1 kg/2¼ lb

1 haggis weighing about 500 g/
1 lb 2 oz

1 egg

2 tbsp chopped fresh flat-leaf
parsley

1 tbsp chopped fresh sage

salt and freshly ground pepper

coarse sea salt

200 g/7 oz carrots, cut into big
chunks

300 g/10 oz leeks, cut into 5 cm/
2 inch pieces

200 g/7 oz medium-size turnips,
quartered

200 g/7 oz celery, cut into 5 cm/
2 inch pieces

1 fresh or 2 dried bay leaves

1 sprig of fresh thyme

8 black peppercorns, coarsely
crushed

1 tsp coriander seeds, coarsely
crushed

300 g/10 oz potatoes, cut into large
cubes

FOR THE HORSERADISH
MAYONNAISE

2 egg yolks

1 tsp Dijon mustard

2 tbsp creamed horseradish

200 ml/7 fl oz olive oil

1 tbsp tarragon vinegar

2 garlic cloves, finely chopped

Ask your butcher to bone out the shoulder, keeping it in one piece.

Skin the haggis and put it in a food processor. Add the egg, parsley and sage and process until this *farce* holds together.

Lay the shoulder on the work surface, boned side up, and season it with salt and pepper. Spread the *farce* over the meat, filling the hollows left by the bones. Roll up the shoulder tightly into a neat bolster shape and secure by tying around at 2 cm/¾ inch intervals with string.

Put the shoulder into a large deep pot, cover it with water and add 1 teaspoon coarse sea salt. Bring to the boil. When boiling point has been reached, lower the heat so the water is simmering and skim all the foam from the surface. Add all the remaining ingredients except the potatoes. Cover and leave to simmer gently for 1 hour. Add the potatoes and simmer for a further 30 minutes.

Meanwhile, make the mayonnaise. Combine the egg yolks, mustard and horseradish in a bowl and whisk together energetically to mix. Still whisking, pour in the oil in a steady stream, a dribble at first and then more quickly. Finish with the vinegar and garlic. Season with salt and pepper.

Lift out the lamb shoulder and set it on a carving board. Wrap it with foil and leave to rest for 10 minutes. Drain all the vegetables and arrange on one side of a large warmed serving platter. Slice the lamb and arrange on the other side of the platter. Add a grinding of black pepper and a sprinkle of sea salt, and serve with the horseradish mayonnaise.

Braised Neck of Lamb with Onions, Peppers and Saffron

Cous d'Agneau Braisé aux Oignons, Poivrons et Safran

---

4 servings

vegetable oil

1.2 kg/2 lb 10 oz middle neck of
    lamb on the bone, cut across
    into 2–2.5 cm/$\frac{3}{4}$–1 inch slices

4 tbsp olive oil

300 g/10 oz onions, chopped

1 red, 1 yellow and 1 green sweet
    pepper, seeded and cut into
    eighths

4 garlic cloves, crushed with the
    side of a knife

1 sprig of fresh thyme

$\frac{1}{2}$ fresh or 1 dried bay leaf

1 tbsp tomato paste

300 ml/10 fl oz white wine

chicken stock or water

a pinch of saffron threads, soaked
    in 1 tbsp water

salt and freshly ground pepper

32 black olives

1 tbsp chopped fresh coriander
    (cilantro)

$\frac{1}{2}$ lemon

Heat a film of vegetable oil in a sauté pan and seal the slices of lamb on both sides. Remove them from the pan and set aside. Add the olive oil to the pan and heat it, then add the onions, sweet peppers, garlic, thyme and bay leaf. Cook, stirring, for 5 minutes. Stir in the tomato paste and white wine, and return the slices of lamb to the pan. Bring to the boil and boil until the liquid has reduced by half.

Add enough chicken stock or water to come level with the ingredients. Add the saffron and stir. Season with salt and pepper. Cover and leave to cook gently for 2 hours or until the meat is tender and is almost falling off the bone.

Before serving, stir in the olives, coriander and a squeeze of lemon and check the seasoning.

- This cut of lamb is one of my favourites because it is so tasty and also one of the cheapest. A bistrot favourite!

- Serve with soft polenta (page 157).

Lambs' Tongues with Red Kidney Beans and Chorizo

Langue d'Agneau aux Haricot Rouge et Chorizo

Offal, or variety meat, has always been a bistrot classic, and I'm sure this will continue to be true as long as these meats are cooked in more interesting ways than they used to be. Let's say goodbye to the bordelaise sauce or the cream and mustard sauce, and hello to tomato and olive relish or beans in red wine with spicy sausage. In my view, these better suit today's tastes. People want more excitement in what they eat, and bistrots should heed that message.

4 servings

12 lambs' tongues

salt

vinegar

200 g/7 oz/1 cup dried red kidney beans

50 g/1¾ oz/3½ tbsp butter

150 g/5 oz chorizo, diced

100 g/3½ oz smoked streaky bacon (thick bacon slices), cut across into large *lardons*

200 g/7 oz carrots, diced

300 g/10 oz button (pearl) onions

3 garlic cloves, chopped

1 bunch of fresh thyme

½ fresh or 1 dried bay leaf

1 bottle of full-bodied red wine, preferably North African

1 beef stock (bouillon) cube, preferably Maggi or Knorr

1 tbsp chopped fresh flat-leaf parsley

The day before, rinse the tongues under cold running water for 5 minutes. Put them in a bowl of cold water and add some ice cubes, a bit of salt and a dash of vinegar. Cover and place in the refrigerator.

Put the kidney beans in a bowl, cover with cold water and leave to soak overnight.

The next day, drain the tongues and put them in a saucepan. Cover with fresh cold water, bring to the boil and boil for 10 minutes. Drain in a colander. When the tongues are cool enough to handle, peel them with the help of a small knife. Set aside.

Drain the beans, put them in a saucepan and cover with water. Bring to the boil and boil for 10 minutes. Drain and set aside.

Melt the butter in a large pot and add the chorizo and bacon. Cook, stirring occasionally, until the fat begins to run, then add the carrots, button onions, garlic, thyme and bay leaf. Cook until the vegetables start to soften. Add the kidney beans and stir well, then add the red wine.

Add the tongues to the pot with the crumbled beef stock cube. There should be enough liquid to cover the ingredients by at least 2 cm/$\frac{3}{4}$ inch, so add some water if necessary. Cover the pot and bring the liquid to simmering point, then leave to cook gently for about 2 hours, stirring with a wooden spoon from time to time.

Before serving, sprinkle with the parsley.

Bruno's notes
- Check from time to time during the simmering and add a little more water if the mixture is looking dry. The liquid should always be level with the ingredients.
- Lambs' tongues can be replaced by cubes of boneless lamb shoulder.

Grilled Lamb Kidneys with a Devilled Sauce

Rognon d'Agneau Grillé, Sauce Diable

12 lambs' kidneys	500 ml/16 fl oz water	**4 servings**
milk	1 garlic clove, crushed with the side	
vegetable oil	of a knife	
75 g/2½ oz/5 tbsp butter	1 bay leaf	
80 g/scant 3 oz shallots, chopped	1 sprig of fresh thyme	
2 tsp brown sugar	1 tbsp sweet mango (Major Grey)	
1 tsp tomato paste	chutney	
½ tsp coriander seeds, coarsely	1 tsp Worcestershire sauce	
crushed	salt and freshly ground pepper	
100 ml/3½ fl oz red wine vinegar	honey or Tabasco sauce (optional)	

Remove any fat covering the kidneys, then peel off the thin membrane. Cut each kidney almost in half, then cut out the core from the centre. Put the kidneys in a bowl and pour over milk to cover. Leave to soak for 3 hours in the refrigerator.

To make the sauce, heat 1 tablespoon oil with 20 g/⅔ oz/1½ tablespoons of the butter in a saucepan. Add the shallots and cook, stirring, until lightly golden and softened. Stir in the sugar and cook for 2 minutes. Add the tomato paste and coriander seeds and cook for a further 2 minutes, stirring well. Stir in the vinegar and water, then add the garlic, bay leaf, thyme, mango chutney and Worcestershire sauce. Leave to simmer for about 45 minutes or until the sauce has reduced by about half. Stir from time to time.

Pass the sauce through a fine sieve into a clean pan, pressing well to be sure all the liquid goes through. Reheat the sauce, then add the remaining butter, cut into pieces, and tilt the pan to melt the butter and swirl it into the sauce. Season with salt and pepper. Taste the sauce: if you find it too sweet, add a dash of vinegar; if too sour, add a tablespoon of honey; if not spicy enough, add a few drops of Tabasco. The sauce should have a good balance between sweet, sour and spicy.

Prepare a charcoal fire or preheat a cast iron ridged grill pan.

Drain the kidneys and pat them dry with paper towels. Thread them on to skewers and brush all over with oil. Grill the kidneys over charcoal, or on the grill pan, turning as necessary, until they are cooked through. Test by cutting into one: a drop of blood should appear.

Reheat the sauce if necessary. Serve the kidneys with the sauce. Sour beetroot (page 148) or mashed potatoes are good accompaniments, as is creamed cauliflower with spring onions (page 145).

Bruno's notes
- Soaking the kidneys in milk will improve their flavour and will also reduce the strong smell they sometimes have.
- The sauce can be prepared in advance, up to the sieving, so the final preparation will take only a few minutes.

Boiled Salted Pork Knuckles with Lentil Salad

Jarret de Porc Bouillie aux Lentilles en Salade

Pork knuckle is a very cheap cut of meat which I like very much, particularly when it is served with a lentil salad and a salsa verde to add acidity and a herby flavour. Surprisingly, this dish can be enjoyed at any time of year.

2 salted pork knuckles (salted ham hocks)	2 garlic cloves, crushed with the side of a knife	**4 servings**
200 g/7 oz carrots	15 black peppercorns, coarsely crushed	
200 g/7 oz onions		
150 g/5 oz celery	200 g/7 oz Puy lentils	
1 sprig of fresh thyme	3 tbsp olive oil dressing (page 205)	
1 bay leaf	freshly ground black pepper	
	salsa verde (page 199), to serve	

Soak the pork knuckles in cold water to cover for 24 hours, changing the water three times. Drain.

Put the pork knuckles in a big pot and cover with plenty of fresh cold water. Bring to the boil, skimming off all the foam that rises to the surface.

Roughly chop the carrots, onions and celery. Add to the pot with the herbs, garlic and peppercorns. Cover and leave to simmer for 3 hours.

Ladle about 1 litre/$1\frac{2}{3}$ pints/1 quart of the cooking liquid from the pot into a saucepan and bring it back to the boil. Add the lentils and cook for 30 minutes or until tender. Drain. Leave the lentils to cool. While they are still warm, toss with the dressing.

Put the lentil salad in a large serving dish. Drain the pork knuckles and cut each into two. Arrange on top of the lentil salad. Grind black pepper over all and serve with the salsa verde.

● Keep the cooking liquid from the pork knuckles and use it as the base for a soup. **Bruno's note**

Mont St Michel Omelette with Black Pudding

Omelette du Mont St Michel au Boudin

The omelette served at La Mère Poulard restaurant, at Mont St Michel in Normandy, has been world famous for many years, and the recipe has been a secret as well guarded as the famous abbey, which was never invaded. I give you here my version of this delicious omelette.

4 servings

12 very fresh free-range eggs
salt and freshly ground pepper
80 g/scant 3 oz/5½ tbsp butter
1 tbsp chopped fresh flat-leaf
   parsley

1 garlic clove, chopped
400 g/14 oz black pudding (blood
   sausage), preferably soft-
   textured, diced
3 tbsp vegetable oil

In a large, wide heatproof bowl set over a pan of boiling water, whisk the eggs until they are pale and thick. Work energetically with the whisk or electric mixer to incorporate as much air as possible. Remove the bowl from over the water and set it on a damp kitchen cloth on the work surface. Continue whisking until the eggs are cold. Season with salt and pepper.

Melt 30 g/1 oz /2 tablespoons of the butter in a pan and add the parsley and garlic. Add the black pudding and heat gently for 5 minutes, stirring frequently.

Heat the remaining butter with the oil in a large non-stick frying pan. When the fat is hot and foaming, pour in the egg mixture. Cook, stirring gently with a wooden spoon, for about 1 minute or until the base is set. Add the black pudding mixture in a line down the centre.

Tilt the pan at a 45° angle and, with the help of a palette knife (metal spatula), fold the omelette over in half. Turn on to a serving dish and serve quickly.

Bruno's note   ● It's a good idea to use a non-stick pan for the omelette, just as a precaution.

Swiss Chard and Black Pudding Tart

Tarte de Blette et Boudin

FOR THE PASTRY

250 g/9 oz/1$\frac{3}{4}$ cups plain (all-
purpose) flour

160 g/5$\frac{1}{2}$ oz/$\frac{3}{4}$ cup soft butter, in
pieces

1 egg

$\frac{1}{2}$ tsp salt

1 tbsp milk

FOR THE FILLING

300 g/10 oz Swiss chard

2 tbsp flour dissolved in a glass of
cold water

$\frac{1}{2}$ lemon

300 ml/10 fl oz double (heavy)
cream

2 eggs

100 g/3$\frac{1}{2}$ oz Emmental cheese,
grated

2 pinches of grated nutmeg

salt and freshly ground black
pepper

250 g/9 oz black pudding (blood
sausage), cut into pieces

6 servings

First make the pastry dough. Put the flour in a bowl and make a well in the centre. Put the pieces of butter in the well and add the egg and salt. Using your fingertips, rub the ingredients together. Add the milk to bind to a dough. Turn the dough on to the work surface. With the palm of your hand, knead the dough to mix it thoroughly until it is no longer sticky. Form into a ball, wrap and chill for 2 hours.

Cut the stalks from the chard leaves; cut the stalks across into slices and set aside. Blanch the chard leaves in boiling salted water for 1 minute, then drain and plunge into cold water. Remove the leaves and squeeze them in your hands to remove all excess water. Roll up the leaves and cut across the rolls into shreds. Set aside.

Bring another saucepan of water to the boil. Add the flour mixture, lemon juice and some salt. Cook the Swiss chard stalks in this mixture for about 5 minutes. Drain in a colander and rinse under cold running water.

In a jug or bowl, mix together the cream, eggs and Emmental. Season with nutmeg, salt and pepper.

On a floured or marble surface, roll out the dough to about 5 mm/$\frac{1}{4}$ inch thick. Use to line a 25 cm/10 inch loose-bottomed tart mould (or you can use a flan ring set on a baking sheet), easing the dough in and trimming off the excess. Prick the tart case all over with a fork. Chill for 20 minutes.

Preheat the oven to 220°C/425°F/Gas 7.

Line the tart case with greaseproof (wax) paper and fill with baking beans. Bake blind for 15 minutes.

Remove the tart case from the oven and lift out the paper and beans. Fill the tart case with the black pudding and the chard stalks and leaves. Place the tart on the pulled-out oven shelf. Pour the cream mixture into the tart case, then slide gently into the oven. Bake for about 20 minutes or until the filling is set.

Remove the side of the tart mould (or lift off the flan ring). Cut the tart into 6 wedges and serve warm, with a side salad.

Bruno's note

● The preparation of salted water and flour is called a *blanc*. It is used for cooking vegetables such as Swiss chard stalks, salsify and artichokes to keep them as white as possible (if they go greyish or brown they don't look very appetizing).

Tripe Stewed with Ginger, Onions and Chilli

Tripes aux Oignons, Chili et Gingembre

1.6 kg/3$\frac{1}{2}$ lb onions

1 red sweet pepper

100 ml/3$\frac{1}{2}$ fl oz olive oil

3 garlic cloves, chopped

1 pig's trotter (optional)

1.2 kg/2 lb 10 oz honeycomb tripe, cut into 4 cm/1$\frac{1}{2}$ inch squares

1 fresh hot red chilli pepper, finely chopped

1 bay leaf

1 sprig of fresh thyme

1 strip of orange zest

2 tsp chopped fresh ginger

2 tsp tomato paste

750 ml/1$\frac{1}{4}$ pints/3 cups dry white wine

salt and freshly ground black pepper

2 tbsp chopped fresh coriander (cilantro)

1 tbsp very small capers

$\frac{1}{2}$ lemon

4 servings

Cut the onions and red pepper into chunks of about 1.5 cm/$\frac{1}{2}$ inch. Heat the olive oil in a large pot and add the onions, red pepper and garlic. Mix well, then cook until the vegetables start to soften a bit. Add the remaining ingredients except the coriander, capers and lemon juice. Bring to the boil. Lower the heat and leave to simmer very gently for 4 hours or until the tripe is tender. To test, squeeze a piece of tripe between two fingers: they should be able to go through.

About 5 minutes before serving, stir in the coriander, capers and lemon juice. Check the seasoning. Add a few drops of virgin olive oil and serve, with plain boiled potatoes.

- If you use a pig's trotter, be sure to take the meat off the bone and to return the meat to the stew for serving.
- To improve the colour of the stew, add a pinch of saffron with the vegetables.

Bruno's notes

VEGETABLES AND GRAINS
(Garnitures)

Monday's Marrow

Courge de Lundi

In my childhood, my family grew all the vegetables for our table. My father used to share an allotment with five other people, one of whom was a Monsieur Charier. He and my father were always comparing the sizes and yields of their vegetables, and they were very competitive about it. One day, my brother had the idea of bringing a mole into M. Charier's garden. That seemed brilliant, until the mole decided to cross the path into our garden! After that the war was on. The result of all this was some very large, 'muscly' vegetables, including some overgrown courgettes that looked like they were on steroids. We ended up with so many that we used to slice them to feed the ducks. My mother would sometimes cook the courgettes on Mondays, stuffed with the leftovers from the Sunday roast. To be honest, I used to prefer the Monday lunch to the Sunday one. The recipe here is a version of that childhood dish, which I sometimes serve at the Bistrot.

---

4 servings

a marrow or similar large squash, weighing about 1.5 kg/3$\frac{1}{3}$ lb

olive oil

200 g/7 oz onions, chopped

60 g/2 oz sun-dried tomatoes (packed in oil), chopped

4 garlic cloves, finely chopped

4 slices of bread

60 g/2 oz firm goat's cheese, preferably *Crottin de Chavignole*, chopped

2 tbsp chopped fresh flat-leaf parsley

400 g/14 oz boneless lamb shoulder, minced (ground)

2 eggs

leaves from 1 sprig of fresh thyme, finely chopped

salt and freshly ground pepper

40 g/1$\frac{1}{2}$ oz Parmesan, freshly grated

1 can (400 g/14 oz) chopped tomatoes with their juice

Preheat the oven to 200°C/400°F/Gas 6.

Cut the marrow in half lengthways. Place the halves in a very large pot or deep roasting pan of boiling salted water and simmer for 5 minutes. Drain and refresh in cold water. With a spoon, scoop out and discard the central seeds and fibres, then scoop out some of the flesh to enlarge the central hollow. Leave the shells at least 1.5 cm/$\frac{1}{2}$ inch thick. Roughly chop the scooped-out flesh.

Heat a film of oil in a frying pan and cook the onions until they are soft.

Add the chopped marrow flesh, sun-dried tomatoes and garlic and cook for about 10 minutes or until all excess liquid has evaporated.

Turn the mixture into a food processor and add the bread, goat's cheese and parsley. Process for 30 seconds. Add the lamb, eggs, thyme and some salt and pepper. Process briefly to mix.

Set the marrow halves, cut sides up, in a roasting pan. Fill with the stuffing and sprinkle with Parmesan. Pour the tomatoes around the marrow and add 3 tablespoons of olive oil. Bake for 45 minutes. After a crust has formed on top of the marrow halves, baste them occasionally with the tomato juice and oil to keep them moist.

Remove the marrow halves from the pan and keep warm. Pour the tomatoes and juices into a blender or food processor and blend until smooth. Press through a fine sieve into a saucepan and reheat.

Slice the marrow and arrange on plates. Spoon the sauce around and add a few drops of virgin olive oil. Serve with a large green salad.

Stuffed Tomato Old-Fashioned Style

Tomate Farcie à l'Ancienne

In summer, when our home-grown tomatoes were abundant, my mother would prepare these stuffed tomatoes in large quantities to freeze in plastic bags. Then, on a winter's night, when spirits were low, we could enjoy this delicious dish. Stuffed tomatoes are very popular in France – even the *charcuteries* have them in their displays. They are regarded as a *dépannage* – a prepared dish to 'help you out' when you don't feel like cooking.

---

4 servings

4 beef tomatoes

3 slices of white bread

milk

4 tbsp olive oil

150 g/5 oz courgettes (zucchini), thinly sliced

150 g/5 oz onions, thinly sliced

500 g/1 lb 2 oz boneless neck of pork, minced (ground)

2 tbsp long-grain rice, cooked in boiling salted water until tender

1 tbsp chopped fresh flat-leaf parsley

2 garlic cloves, finely chopped

1 egg, beaten

salt and freshly ground pepper

2 pinches of sugar

1 tsp tomato paste

Preheat the oven to 200°C/400°F/Gas 6.

Cut a thin slice off the top of each tomato; reserve these tops. Using a teaspoon, scoop out the pulp and seeds into a small bowl. Sprinkle the inside of each tomato with a little salt. Turn them upside down and leave to drain on paper towels.

Briefly work the tomato pulp and seeds in a blender, then strain through a sieve and reserve.

Put the bread in a bowl and add enough milk to moisten, mashing with a fork to make a paste. Heat half of the oil in a frying pan and cook the courgettes and onions for 4 minutes. Turn the fried vegetables into a bowl and add the pork, rice, bread paste, parsley, garlic and egg. Season with salt and pepper. Mix well with a large wooden spoon.

Fill the tomatoes with the pork mixture. Arrange them in a small roasting pan. Mix the strained tomato pulp with the sugar and tomato paste and pour into the pan around the tomatoes. Sprinkle the remaining olive oil over the tomatoes. Bake for 5 minutes, then reduce the oven temperature to 140°C/275°F/Gas 1 and continue baking for 30 minutes. Halfway through, put the reserved tops back on the tomatoes.

Serve the tomatoes hot.

Bruno's notes

- If you like, you can serve the cooking juice with the tomatoes. If it is too liquid (because of the juices the tomatoes will give), boil to reduce it, stirring well.
- Serve with a green salad mixed with French (thin green) beans.

Potato Cakes

Gâteaux de Pomme de Terre

600 g/1¼ lb potatoes, such as
   Desirée or King Edwards
60 g/2 oz/4 tbsp butter
1 garlic clove, finely chopped
1 tbsp chopped fresh flat-leaf
   parsley
salt and freshly ground pepper

flour
1 egg yolk
2 tbsp water
100 g/3½ oz/1 cup flaked (sliced)
   almonds
2 tbsp vegetable oil

4 servings

Peel the potatoes and cut into large cubes. Put them in a large saucepan, cover with water and add 1 teaspoon salt. Bring to the boil, then simmer until the potatoes are soft and cooked but not mushy. Drain in a colander. Spread the potatoes in a baking tray and dry them off in the oven set at a very low temperature. When the potatoes are very dry, work them through a vegetable mill or potato ricer into a bowl. Add half of the butter and beat it in until melted, then add the garlic and parsley and season with salt and pepper. Leave to cool completely.

On a lightly floured surface roll the potato mixture to a cylindrical shape. Cut across into four equal portions. Flatten each portion to a disc about 2.5 cm/1 inch thick.

Have three plates ready in front of you, one with flour, one with the egg yolk beaten with the water and 2 pinches of salt, and one with the flaked almonds. Coat each potato cake lightly in flour, shaking off excess, then dip into the egg mixture and, finally, coat with flaked almonds. Chill for 20–30 minutes to set the coating.

Heat the oil and remaining butter in a large frying pan. Cook the potato cakes gently until they are golden brown on both sides and piping hot. Serve hot.

Bruno's note
● You can prepare and coat the potato cakes in advance, then keep them refrigerated until you are ready to cook them. Alternatively, colour them on both side and leave them to cool, then cover and refrigerate. About 5 minutes before serving, arrange them on a baking sheet and put them under the grill (broiler) to heat up, turning once, or reheat in the oven.

Sliced Potatoes
Baked in Cream with Garlic

Gratin Dauphinois

The French pharmacist and agronomist, Antoine Augustin Parmentier, was an enthusiastic propagandist for the potato, having discovered its nutritional value when he was in the French army during the Seven Years War. With the support of Louis XVI he was able to plant potatoes all around Paris – even the beautiful *Jardin des Tuileries* was turned into a potato field. So this vegetable which the French had considered to be indigestible and fit only for cattle feed became a revered staple of the cuisine.

---

200 ml/7 fl oz milk

200 ml/7 fl oz double (heavy) cream

salt and freshly ground pepper

2 pinches of freshly grated nutmeg

1 kg/$2\frac{1}{4}$ lb potatoes, cut into 5 mm/$\frac{1}{4}$ inch slices

60 g/2 oz/4 tbsp soft unsalted butter

3 garlic cloves, very finely chopped

4 servings

Preheat the oven to 180°C/350°F/Gas 4.

Boil the milk, then pour it into a large bowl and stir in the cream. Season with salt and pepper and add the nutmeg. Add the potato slices and mix well.

Spread the soft butter all over the inside of a gratin dish, then sprinkle the garlic evenly over the butter. Layer the potato slices in the dish, overlapping them slightly. Finally, pour in the milk and cream mixture.

Place the dish in the oven and bake for about 45 minutes or until the potatoes are tender (test with the tip of a sharp knife) and the top is golden. Serve hot.

Lyonnaise Potatoes

Pommes Lyonnaise

This dish is found in every bistrot in Lyon. I have changed the traditional recipe slightly by not peeling the potatoes (the skin gives a good flavour) and by adding some bacon.

4 servings

40 g/1½ oz/3 tbsp butter

300 g/10 oz onions, thinly sliced

120 g/4 oz streaky bacon (thick bacon slices), cut across into *lardons*

2 garlic cloves, finely chopped

1.2 kg/2 lb 10 oz new potatoes with smooth skin, washed but not peeled

5 tbsp vegetable oil

1 tbsp chopped fresh flat-leaf parsley

Melt the butter in a heavy pan and cook the onions with the *lardons* until they are soft and lightly browned. Stir in the chopped garlic. Cover the pan, remove from the heat and set aside.

Cut the potatoes into 3 mm/⅛ inch slices. Rinse the slices in cold water, then pat dry completely with paper towels.

Heat the vegetable oil in a frying pan. When it is hot, add the potatoes and fry until they are tender and golden brown on both sides, turning them with a wooden spatula. Add the onion mixture and stir to mix. Cover the pan, lower the heat and cook for 5 minutes, stirring once or twice.

Just before serving, sprinkle with parsley.

Mashed potatoes are everyone's favourite, but the fashion for nursery food has muddled the precise use for this vegetable dish. Mashed potatoes go beautifully with stews and rich sauces, but not with grilled fish!

Mashed Potatoes

Purée de Pommes de Terre

800 g/1¾ lb potatoes, peeled and cut into chunks

150 g/5 oz/10 tbsp cold unsalted butter, cut into small pieces

salt

150 ml/5 fl oz hot milk

freshly grated nutmeg

4 servings

Preheat the oven to 180°C/350°F/Gas 4.

Put the potatoes in a saucepan and cover with cold water. Add a little salt. Bring to the boil and simmer gently until the potatoes are soft – about 25 minutes depending on the quality of the potatoes. Test them with the tip of a sharp knife.

Drain the potatoes in a colander and spread them out in a roasting pan. Put into the oven to dry for 10 minutes.

Pass the potatoes through a vegetable mill (mouli) or potato ricer into a clean saucepan. Add the butter a few pieces at a time, stirring with a wooden spoon. Slowly pour in the hot milk, stirring well, then season with 2 pinches of nutmeg. Serve hot.

Bruno's notes

● Potatoes for mashing should have a floury texture. I think that the best British varieties are Desirée, Pentland Crown and Pentland Hawk.

● Some people like their mash more runny – just add more milk or cream.

Fondant Potatoes

These make a change from traditional roast potatoes on Sunday.

Pommes Fondantes

---

4 servings

4 potatoes, each weighing about 250 g/9 oz

2 tbsp vegetable oil

500 ml/16 fl oz chicken stock, or use 250 ml/8 fl oz each poultry *jus* (page 195) and water

2 garlic cloves, chopped

1 sprig of fresh rosemary

60 g/2 oz/4 tbsp butter

salt

Preheat the oven to 160°C/325°F/Gas 3.

Peel the potatoes and cut each into a barrel shape. Cut the barrels in half lengthwise to make pieces 6–7 cm/2½–3 inches long.

Heat the oil in a small roasting pan on top of the stove. Put the potatoes in the pan and brown lightly on all sides, turning to colour evenly.

Pour the stock or *jus* and water mixture into the pan and add the garlic and rosemary. Put a piece of butter on top of each potato and sprinkle with a little salt. Put into the oven and leave to cook for 30 minutes or until the liquid has evaporated and the potatoes are tender. Test them with a sharp knife: there should be no resistance. During the cooking, spoon the liquid over the potatoes about five times to glaze them and give them a nice colour. When done they will be deep golden brown and shiny.

French Fries

Pommes de Terre Frites

1.35 kg/3 lb potatoes	fine salt	**4 servings**
groundnut (peanut) oil for deep frying	coarse sea salt	

Peel the potatoes, then square them with a knife on a chopping board. Cut into 1 cm/$\frac{3}{8}$ inch slices and cut each slice into sticks. Put the potatoes into a basin of cold water and rinse them very well. Drain and pat dry on a kitchen cloth.

Heat oil to 130°C/265°F in a deep pan.

Put the potatoes in a frying basket and fry them in the oil until they become slightly soft (test by removing one, cooling it and then squeezing it between two fingers: it should still have some resistance). Drain the potatoes.

Reheat the oil to 180°C/350°F. Lower the basket of potatoes back into the oil and fry until golden and crisp. Drain the potatoes very well in the basket or on paper towels. Tip the potatoes on to a paper napkin in a dish and season with fine salt and coarse sea salt. Serve immediately.

New Potatoes with Almonds

Pommes Nouvelles aux Amandes

4 servings

600 g/1¼ lb new potatoes

40 g/1½ oz/3 tbsp butter

60 g/2 oz/⅔ cup flaked (sliced) almonds

1 tbsp chopped fresh chives or spring onions (scallions)

coarse sea salt

pepper

Cook the potatoes in boiling salted water until they are just tender (test with the point of a knife). Drain well in a colander.

Heat the butter in a frying pan, add the almonds and cook gently until golden brown, stirring frequently. Add the potatoes and toss to coat with the butter and almonds. Sprinkle in the chives.

Quickly turn into a serving dish, sprinkle the top with sea salt and freshly ground black pepper, and serve.

Bruno's note

● Use Jersey Royal potatoes when they are in season.

Smooth Broccoli Purée

Purée de Brocoli

800 g/1¾ lb broccoli florets
½ garlic clove, finely chopped
100 ml/3½ fl oz olive oil

salt and freshly ground white
pepper

4 servings

Cook the broccoli florets in boiling salted water until you can pierce them easily with a knife blade. Drain well in a colander, then transfer to a food processor. Add the garlic and olive oil and process until smooth. Season with salt and pepper.

Reheat the purée gently for serving, stirring constantly.

● You can peel and slice the broccoli stalks and then cook them in boiling salted water. **Bruno's note**
Just before serving, toss in butter with chopped parsley.

Spinach with Almonds and Nutmeg

Epinard aux Amandes et Noix de Muscade

---

4 servings

1 kg/2¼ lb fresh spinach, trimmed

olive oil

50 g/1⅔ oz/½ cup flaked (sliced)
   almonds or pine kernels (nuts)

salt and pepper

freshly grated nutmeg

Clean the spinach thoroughly in cold water, changing the water at least three times. Lift it into a colander to drain, but don't pat it dry.

Heat 2 tablespoons oil in a large pot and add the almonds, 3 pinches of salt and 2 large pinches of nutmeg. Cook until the almonds just start to colour. Add the spinach and cook for 30 seconds, then turn the spinach over with a wooden spoon so the top leaves are at the bottom. Cook for a further 3 minutes or until the spinach is wilted and tender. Test a leaf to see.

Drain in a colander to remove excess water, then turn into a serving dish. Add a few drops of olive oil and season with freshly ground black pepper.

Bruno's notes

- When buying spinach, make sure the leaves are crisp and green. These days good spinach with a nice iron flavour is quite rare, so be selective.

- Cooking spinach this way, rather than in boiling water, will retain the maximum flavour.

Peas French-style

Petit Pois à la Française

When my mother used to roast young squab for dinner, only one vegetable dish seemed to be an acceptable garnish: *petit pois à la française*. I don't know whether this was tradition or taste, but we never complained because it was so good. The sweet fresh flavour of young peas from our garden became magical when blended with onions, lettuce, garlic and fresh thyme.

---

1 kg/2¼ lb fresh peas

90 g/3 oz/6 tbsp butter

100 g/3½ oz streaky bacon (thick bacon slices), cut across into *lardons*

150 g/5 oz new white onions, sliced

1 tsp fresh thyme leaves

1 garlic clove, chopped

1 round (Boston or bibb) lettuce, finely shredded

¼ Maggi chicken stock (bouillon) cube

freshly ground black pepper

150 ml/5 fl oz water

2 tsp cornflour (cornstarch) mixed with 1 tbsp water

2 tbsp chopped fresh chives

4 servings

Remove the peas from the pods. Blanch them in boiling salted water for 2 minutes. Drain well, refresh in cold water and set aside.

Melt 30 g/1 oz/2 tablespoons of the butter in a large saucepan. Add the bacon and onions and cook gently for 3–4 minutes, stirring frequently. Add the thyme, garlic, lettuce and stock cube and mix well with a wooden spoon. Season with pepper. Add the peas with the water and leave to simmer for 5 minutes.

Add the cornflour mixture to the peas and stir well, then cook over a low heat for a further 5 minutes

Just before serving, add the remaining butter and the chives and tilt the pan to melt the butter and swirl it into the mixture.

● You can use frozen petit pois, thawed and drained, instead of fresh peas, but buy the very small ones. They won't need the initial blanching.   **Bruno's note**

Grilled Aubergine Purée

Aubergine 'Biste'

*B*iste is an old provençal name for an aubergine and tomato purée. The modern version here can be served as a starter or as a vegetable garnish.

8 or more servings

1 kg/2¼ lb aubergines (eggplants)
salt and freshly ground pepper
1 kg/2¼ lb plum-type tomatoes
olive oil

4 garlic cloves, chopped
½ tbsp fresh marjoram leaves
vegetable oil

Cut the aubergines lengthwise into slices about 1.5 cm/½ inch thick. Lay them on a tray in one layer and sprinkle with salt. Cover and leave to drain for at least 1 hour.

Meanwhile, plunge the tomatoes into boiling water and blanch for 5 seconds, then remove and refresh immediately in iced water. Slip off the skins. Cut the tomatoes in half and squeeze out all the seeds. Chop the flesh roughly.

Prepare a charcoal fire, or preheat a ridged cast iron grill pan.

Heat 4 tablespoons of olive oil in a large saucepan. Add the garlic and stir, then add the tomatoes and marjoram. Leave to stew gently while you finish the aubergines.

Rinse the aubergine slices under cold running water and pat dry. Brush them on both sides with mixed olive oil and vegetable oil. Grill the slices over hot charcoal or on the grill pan until coloured on both sides and starting to soften. Then chop the slices roughly. Add to the tomato mixture and leave to stew for about 30 minutes, stirring occasionally.

Check the seasoning before serving, hot or cold.

Bruno's note

● This recipe will make quite a large quantity, but all excess can be stored in a jar, covered with a film of olive oil, in the refrigerator for up to a week.

Creamed Cauliflower with Spring Onions

Chou-fleur en Bèchamel et Oignons Nouveaux

650 g/1 lb 7 oz cauliflower florets

250 ml/8 fl oz milk

30 g/1 oz/2 tbsp butter

$\frac{1}{2}$ tbsp flour

freshly grated nutmeg

salt and freshly ground pepper

2 tbsp crème fraîche

4 spring onions (scallions), finely
chopped

60 g/2 oz Gruyère cheese, grated

4 servings

Blanch the cauliflower florets in boiling salted water for 1 minute. Drain in a colander and return to the pan. Add the milk, bring to the boil and simmer until the cauliflower is tender but still firm (al dente).

Meanwhile, in another saucepan, melt the butter. When the butter starts to foam (do not let it turn colour), add the flour and mix well. Cook for 1 minute, stirring; the mixture (*roux*) will start to turn white. Remove from the heat and allow the *roux blanc* to cool.

When the cauliflower is cooked, drain it in a colander set in a bowl. Add the hot milk to the *roux blanc* and mix well with a whisk. Season with nutmeg, salt and pepper to taste. Bring to the boil and simmer gently for 20 minutes, stirring occasionally.

Preheat the oven to 220°C/425°F/Gas 7.

Stir the crème fraîche and spring onions into the sauce. Fold in the cauliflower. Put into a buttered gratin dish and sprinkle the cheese over the top. Bake for 15 minutes. If necessary, finish under the grill (broiler) to brown the top lightly. Serve hot.

Ratatouille

This famous dish from Provence is basically a vegetable stew. But the vegetables do not all need the same cooking time, so it is important to add them in stages. Some people like to add some black olives – the small Niçoise olives in particular – but this is optional. Ratatouille is served warm as a vegetable garnish, or cold as a dish on its own with a little extra virgin olive oil on the top.

4–6 servings

200 g/7 oz ripe plum-type tomatoes	salt and pepper
200 g/7 oz courgettes (zucchini)	1 sprig of fresh thyme
250 g/9 oz onions	$\frac{1}{2}$ bay leaf
150 g/5 oz red sweet pepper, seeded	1 sprig of fresh rosemary
150 g/5 oz yellow sweet pepper, seeded	3 garlic cloves, finely chopped
200 g/7 oz aubergine (eggplant)	$\frac{1}{2}$ tbsp chopped fresh parsley
3 tbsp olive oil	5 fresh basil leaves, shredded with scissors
	extra virgin olive oil to finish

Immerse the tomatoes in a pan of boiling water, leave for 30 seconds and then refresh in iced water. Drain and peel off the skin. Cut each tomato into quarters and set aside.

Cut the courgettes, onions, peppers and aubergine into 2 cm/$\frac{3}{4}$ inch cubes.

Heat the olive oil in a large heavy pot (Le Creuset type), add the courgettes and fry quickly for 1 minute, stirring, to soften a bit. With a slotted spoon, remove the courgettes and set aside.

Put the onions and sweet peppers in the pot. Lower the heat to moderate and stir well to mix the vegetables with the oil. Add 3 pinches of salt, the thyme, bay leaf, rosemary and garlic. Cook for about 5 minutes or until the vegetables are soft, stirring occasionally. Add the aubergine and stir to mix. Cook for a further 2 minutes, then add the tomatoes. Stir in $\frac{1}{3}$ glass of water and cover the pot. Leave to cook for 5 minutes. Return the courgettes to the pot, stir and cook, covered, for a further 5 minutes.

Just before serving, stir in the parsley and basil, check the seasoning and add a splash of extra virgin olive oil.

BOUDIN BLANC WITH ONION GRAVY, *PAGE 98*

BOILED SALTED PORK KNUCKLE WITH LENTIL SALAD, *PAGE 123*

- If you are serving the ratatouille with grilled fish, add 5 canned anchovy fillets, finely chopped. This is superb!
- With roast lamb, add some goat's cheese to the ratatouille just before serving.

Broad Bean and Lovage Purée

Purée de Fèves à la Livèche

Let's be honest. Fresh broad beans are nice only for a short period in the summer, and most of the time the shell is half empty. So, like me, use good frozen ones.

2.2 kg/$4\frac{3}{4}$ lb fresh broad (fava) beans in shell or 750 g/$1\frac{1}{2}$ lb frozen broad beans, thawed	50 g/$1\frac{2}{3}$ oz/$3\frac{1}{2}$ tbsp butter	**4 servings**
	1 garlic clove, finely chopped	
	$\frac{1}{2}$ Maggi chicken stock (bouillon) cube	
100 ml/$3\frac{1}{2}$ fl oz double (heavy) cream	1 tsp chopped fresh lovage	
	salt and pepper	

If you are using fresh broad beans, remove them from the shells, then blanch for 1 minute in boiling salted water. When the beans are cool enough to handle, squeeze the beans out of their skins.

Combine the cream, butter, garlic and stock cube in a saucepan and bring to the boil. Stir in the beans, then lower the heat and cook for 8 minutes or until very tender. Pour the mixture into a food processor and process until smooth.

Return the purée to the pan. Add the lovage and season with salt and pepper. Reheat gently for serving.

- This purée is my favourite garnish with roast duck – the slightly bitter yet sweet flavour complements duck perfectly.
- Take care when adding salt as the stock cube may provide enough.

Sour Beetroot

Betteraves Aigres

4 servings

600 g/1$\frac{1}{4}$ lb raw medium-size beetroots (beets)

3$\frac{1}{2}$ tbsp red wine vinegar

2 tsp roughly chopped fresh sage

5 tbsp water

2 tbsp soured cream

2 garlic cloves, finely chopped

$\frac{1}{2}$ tbsp chopped fresh dill

salt and freshly ground pepper

Preheat the oven to 190°C/375°F/Gas 5.

Clean the beetroots well and put them on a large, doubled sheet of foil. Add the vinegar, sage and water. Wrap up the foil around the beetroots to make a tight parcel and place it in a roasting pan. Bake for 30 minutes or until the beetroots are tender. Test by inserting the tip of a sharp knife into a beetroot.

When the beetroots are cooked, unwrap and drain them, then peel using your thumb. Cut each beetroot into quarters. Put them in a microwave-safe serving dish.

Just before serving, reheat the beetroots in the microwave for a few seconds, then add the soured cream, garlic, dill and some salt and pepper. Toss and serve.

Bruno's notes

- This goes extremely well with red meat and game, but is also surprisingly good with grilled mackerel.
- If you don't have a microwave, reheat the beetroot with a few drops of water in a covered pan.
- Preparing beetroot this way is much more tasty than cooking them in boiling water.

Braised Red Cabbage with Caraway Seeds

Choux Rouge Braisé au Graines de Carvi

1 kg/2¼ lb red cabbage

45 g/1½ oz/3 tbsp butter

¼ tsp caraway seeds

1 bay leaf

2 garlic cloves, finely chopped

200 g/7 oz onions, finely chopped

150 g/5 oz green apple, such as
   Granny Smith, peeled, cored and
   thinly sliced

2 tbsp redcurrant jelly

125 ml/4 fl oz red wine vinegar

300 ml/10 fl oz water

salt and freshly ground pepper

4 servings

Cut the cabbage into quarters and cut out the hard core. Shred the quarters finely.

Melt the butter in a large heavy saucepan and stir in the caraway seeds, bay leaf and garlic. Add the onions and apple and cook for 3–4 minutes, stirring occasionally. Add the cabbage and redcurrant jelly and mix well, then add the vinegar, water and salt and pepper to taste.

Cover the pan with a sheet of buttered greaseproof (wax) paper and then the lid. Leave to cook over a low heat for 1 hour or until the cabbage is tender, stirring from time to time. Discard the bay leaf and check the seasoning before serving.

Potted Cabbage and Lardons

Etouffé de Chou au Lardons

4 servings

600 g/1¼ lb Savoy cabbage

80 g/scant 3 oz/6 tbsp duck fat or butter

120 g/4 oz smoked streaky bacon (thick bacon slices), cut across into *lardons*

100 g/3½ oz onions, cut into 5 mm/ ¼ inch dice

120 g/4 oz turnips, cut into 5 mm/ ¼ inch dice

1 tsp chopped fresh sage

2 garlic cloves, finely chopped

salt and pepper

Shred the cabbage quite finely. Blanch it in boiling salted water for 30 seconds, then drain and refresh under cold running water.

Melt the duck fat or butter in a large heavy pan and add the *lardons*, onions, turnips, sage and garlic. Mix well, then add the cabbage. Season with a little salt and pepper. Mix again and add ½ glass of water. Cover and leave to cook over a low heat for about 30 minutes or until the cabbage is tender, stirring occasionally.

Check the seasoning before serving.

Bruno's note   ● Be cautious when adding salt because the bacon may be very salty.

H ere the cabbage is not fermented, but takes on quite an interesting flavour.

Sour Cabbage

Choucroute

800 g/1¾ lb white cabbage	16 juniper berries	**4 servings**
2 tbsp coarse sea salt	2 bay leaves	
750 ml/1¼ pints/3 cups white wine from Germany or Alsace	3 pinches of white pepper	

Cut the cabbage into quarters and cut out the core. Slice the cabbage as finely as possible and put it in a bowl. Sprinkle the cabbage with the salt and rub in your hands, pressing firmly, for 5 minutes. Cover the cabbage with a plate and put a 900 g/2 lb weight on top (such as two cans of food). Leave at room temperature for 3 hours.

Turn the cabbage into a sieve or colander and rinse well under cold running water.

Combine the wine, juniper berries and bay leaves in a pot and add the cabbage. Season with the pepper. Cover and cook over a low heat for about 1 hour or until the cabbage is tender, stirring from time to time.

● An electric slicing machine or fine shredding disc on a food processor will slice the cabbage very finely.   **Bruno's note**

Pumpkin and Parmesan Purée

Purée de Potiron au Parmesan

---

4 servings

1.2 kg/2 lb 10 oz pumpkin

160 g/5$\frac{1}{2}$ oz/11 tbsp butter

salt and freshly ground pepper

1 garlic clove, peeled

1 tsp chopped fresh sage

2 tbsp freshly grated Parmesan

Preheat the oven to 130°C/250°F/Gas $\frac{1}{2}$.

Cut the pumpkin into four pieces. Scoop out and discard the central seeds and fibres. Put the pieces of pumpkin, flesh up, in a roasting pan. Dot with 100 g/3$\frac{1}{2}$ oz/7 tablespoons of the butter, cut into pieces, and season with salt and pepper. Pour enough cold water into the pan to make a 2.5 cm/ 1 inch layer. Bake for 1–2 hours or until the pumpkin is very soft and collapsed.

Meanwhile, blanch the garlic clove in a small pan of boiling water three times, using fresh water for each blanching. Drain well.

Melt the remaining butter in a small pan and heat until it turns the colour of hazelnut shells (*noisette*).

Scoop all the pumpkin flesh from the skin and put it into a food processor. Add the garlic, noisette butter and sage. Process until smooth. If the purée seems too liquid, pour it into a pan and cook to evaporate excess moisture.

Taste and add salt and pepper, then stir in the Parmesan.

Pearl Barley and Pumpkin 'Like a Risotto'

Orge Perlé et Potiron Comme une Risotto

What I like most about this dish is that it uses often neglected ingredients. The 'risotto' makes an interesting and unusual accompaniment to white meat.

---

450 g/1 lb piece of pumpkin
(weight without seeds and fibres)
$3\frac{1}{2}$ tbsp vegetable oil
160 g/$5\frac{1}{2}$ oz/$\frac{3}{4}$ cup pearl barley

50 g/$1\frac{2}{3}$ oz/$3\frac{1}{2}$ tbsp butter
1 tbsp chopped fresh chives
salt and freshly ground pepper

4 servings

Preheat the oven to 170°C/325°F/Gas 3.

Put the piece of pumpkin, flesh up, in a small roasting pan. Pour the vegetable oil and a glass of water into the pan. Bake for about 30 minutes or until the pumpkin flesh is very soft and collapsed to about a third of the initial volume.

Meanwhile, put the barley in a saucepan and add enough water to come 3 cm/$1\frac{1}{4}$ inches above it. Bring to the boil and simmer until tender. Drain in a colander and return to the pan.

Spoon the pumpkin flesh out of the skin and chop it roughly on a chopping board. Add to the barley with the butter. Heat gently, stirring, until piping hot. Just before serving, stir in the chives and season with salt and pepper.

● If you are health conscious you can replace the butter with olive oil.

Bruno's note

Green Lentils Flavoured with Cardamom

Lentilles Vertes, du Puy, à la Cardamom

The small Le Puy lentils from the Auvergne, in the centre of France, bear an *appellation d'origine* which, like the appellations given to fine wines, guarantees that they are genuinely from this particular region and have been grown according to stringent standards – including cultivation without fertilizers. Le Puy lentils have a delicate taste and a fine green skin. They are much appreciated by chefs.

4 servings

100 g/3½ oz onions

150 g/5 oz carrots

100 g/3½ oz celery

olive oil

8 rashers smoked streaky bacon (thick bacon slices), cut across into *lardons*

2 garlic cloves, finely chopped

½ bay leaf

6 cardamom pods, crushed with the base of a heavy pan

250 g/9 oz Le Puy lentils

800 ml/1⅓ pints/3¼ cups water

50 g/scant 2 oz/3½ tbsp butter or duck fat

1 tbsp chopped fresh coriander (cilantro)

salt and pepper

Cut the onions, carrots and celery into 1.5 cm/⅝ inch dice. Heat a film of oil in a heavy pan. Add the diced vegetables, *lardons*, garlic, bay leaf and cardamom and stir well. Cook for about 5 minutes, stirring occasionally.

Add the lentils and pour in the water. Bring to the boil, then lower the heat and leave to simmer for 30 minutes or until the lentils are tender.

Stir in the butter or duck fat and coriander. Season with salt and pepper. Serve hot.

Bruno's note

● After crushing the cardamom pods, tip into the palm of your hand and shake gently. The pieces of pod can be easily separated and removed from the black seeds.

Split Pea Purée with Parsley

Purée de Pois Cassés au Persil

---

320 g/11 oz/1$\frac{1}{2}$ cups dried split peas
chicken stock or water
100 ml/3$\frac{1}{2}$ fl oz double (heavy)
  cream

1 tbsp chopped blanched flat-leaf
  parsley
50 g/1$\frac{2}{3}$ oz/3$\frac{1}{2}$ tbsp butter
salt and freshly ground pepper

4 servings

Put the split peas in a saucepan and pour in enough chicken stock or water to come 3 cm/1$\frac{1}{4}$ inches above the peas. Bring to the boil, then leave to simmer for 40 minutes or until tender.

Meanwhile, bring the cream to the boil in a small saucepan. Add the parsley. Pour into a blender (or use a hand-held blender) and blend to a smooth green cream. Set aside.

When the peas are cooked, turn into a food processor (there should be no need to drain them). Add the butter and parsley cream and season with salt and pepper. Process until smooth. Reheat for serving.

- The reason for blanching the parsley is so its flavour will be absorbed more fully by the cream. Also the resulting mixture will have a richer green colour.
- If you find the purée too thick, add some hot milk.
- I like this purée topped with garlic butter: melt some butter and cook a little finely chopped garlic until it is golden. Pour this over the purée.

Bruno's notes

Red Kidney Bean Purée

Purée de Haricot Rouge

4 servings

200 g/7 oz/1 cup dried red kidney beans, soaked overnight and drained

4 tbsp olive oil

100 g/3½ oz carrots, cut into 1.5 cm/⅝ inch dice

100 g/3½ oz onions, cut into 1.5 cm/⅝ inch dice

2 garlic cloves, crushed with the side of a knife

1 bouquet garni (page 209)

½ Maggi chicken stock (bouillon) cube

salt and pepper

1 tbsp chopped fresh coriander (cilantro)

Put the kidney beans in a saucepan, cover with cold water and bring to the boil. Boil for 10 minutes, then drain and set aside.

Heat half of the olive oil in a heavy saucepan. Add the carrots, onions, garlic and bouquet garni and sweat the vegetables over a low heat, covered, until they are very soft. Add the kidney beans and stock cube. Pour in enough water to come 3 cm/1¼ inches above the level of the ingredients. Bring to the boil, skimming off the foam from the surface, then leave to simmer for 2 hours.

Remove from the heat and leave to cool completely. Drain the beans and vegetables, reserving the cooking liquid.

Purée the beans and vegetables in a food processor, adding enough of the reserved liquid to give the right consistency. Press the purée through a sieve set over a bowl. Put into a clean pan and reheat. Season with salt and pepper. Add the coriander and remaining olive oil, mix well and serve.

Soft Polenta

Polente

800 ml/1⅓ pints/3 cups water

salt

200 g/7 oz/1 cup polenta

50 g/scant 2 oz/3½ tbsp butter

1 tbsp chopped parsley

1 tsp chopped fresh sage

1 tbsp freshly grated Parmesan

olive oil

4 servings

Bring the salted water to the boil. Gradually add the polenta, stirring constantly with a wooden spoon. Cook for 5 minutes, stirring.

Add the butter, herbs and Parmesan. Serve immediately, drizzled with a few drops of olive oil.

● If you like, top the polenta with some cooked tomato sauce (page 200).

Bruno's note

DESSERTS AND BAKING

Monsieur Lopez's Almond Cake

Gâteau Basque Maison Lopez

In French bistrots, the choice of desserts is quite limited and they are often boring due to a lack of attention. I must admit that I don't have much of a sweet tooth, but I have always thought about the end of a meal as seriously as the start. This is probably due to the influence of one of my first teachers.

At the age of 13 I decided that it was time to start my culinary training, with experience in the different areas – pastry chef, *charcutier*, and so on. Libourne, where I was born and brought up, was lucky to have a Master Pâtissier named Manuel Lopez. His work was so highly respected that people travelled even from Bordeaux, 20 miles away, to purchase his beautiful cakes, chocolates and ice creams. So you can understand that for me the first choice for work experience was with M. Lopez, and I found a place with him during the school holidays.

On the first day of my two-week *stage* in M. Lopez's kitchen, he offered me some pastry for breakfast.

When I had finished my two pains au chocolat and my three croissants, he pushed me to have more, dipped in chocolate sauce! As you can imagine I was quite full and more than content. In fact, I was feeling slightly unwell. One of his pâtissiers explained to me that M. Lopez did that with all newcomers, to make sure they would not eat up all his profits!

M. Lopez was quite a character. At 1.7 metres (5 ft 5½ in) in height and 100 kilos (15½ st), he had real authority in the 'laboratory'. I greatly admired his control of everything that was going on and his demands for perfection. He had the respect of all who worked for him. He has now retired, leaving his son to run the pastry shop, and is enjoying his new hobby, cooking, in his beautiful home in Bordeaux. He has promised me that he will come to London for a two-week *stage* at my new restaurant, L'Odéon. Twenty years later I will have the privilege of showing him my work.

---

6 servings

FOR THE DOUGH

2 eggs

2 tbsp rum

2 pinches of salt

200 g/7 oz/1 cup caster (granulated) sugar

200 g/7 oz/1¼ cups plain (all-purpose) flour

200 g/7 oz/14 tbsp very soft unsalted butter

100 g/3½ oz/1⅓ cups ground almonds

1 egg yolk beaten with 2 tsp water, to glaze

Prepare the dough for the gâteau 48 hours before baking, to give it time to firm up. Put the egg, rum, salt and sugar in a mixing bowl and mix well with a whisk until the mixture starts to turn white and foamy. Add the remaining ingredients, except the egg yolk wash, and mix energetically with a wooden spatula to make a smooth dough. Place in the refrigerator.

FOR THE CRÈME PÂTISSIÈRE

150 ml/5 fl oz milk

$3\frac{1}{2}$ tbsp double (heavy) cream

$\frac{1}{2}$ vanilla pod (bean), split open

2 egg yolks

50 g/scant 2 oz/$\frac{1}{4}$ cup caster
(granulated) sugar

1 tbsp flour

bitter almond essence (extract) to
flavour

To make the *crème pâtissière*, put the milk, cream and vanilla pod in a heavy saucepan and bring just to the boil. Meanwhile, mix together the egg yolks and sugar in a bowl, then add the flour. Pour the hot milk mixture over the egg yolk mixture, mixing well. Pour back into the saucepan. Cook on a low heat for 20 minutes, stirring frequently. Pour the *crème pâtissière* into a shallow dish and leave to cool completely.

When the *crème* is cold, flavour it with the almond essence, adding just a little – a drop on the end of a knife blade is enough.

When you are ready to bake the gâteau, preheat the oven to 180°C/ 350°F/Gas 4.

Roll out just over half of the dough to 1 cm/$\frac{3}{8}$ inch thick and use to line a 23 cm/9 inch tart mould. Fill with the *crème pâtissière*. Roll out the remaining dough thinly and use to cover the top. Seal the edges together. Brush the top of the gâteau with the egg yolk wash.

Bake for 25–30 minutes or until golden brown. The gâteau is best served at room temperature, with raspberry jam.

Orange and Cardamom Rice Pudding

Riz au Lait à l'Orange et Cardamom

I love the flavours of orange and cardamom together. For quite a few years now I have used this combination in many dishes, mainly shellfish, but also in puddings and especially in rice pudding. My mother used to cook rice pudding with dried orange zest – she dried the zest by hanging it in the kitchen, and I remember how fragrant it was. We always ate the delicious creamy pudding cold in breakfast bowls.

4 servings

50 g/1¾ oz/¼ cup short-grain pudding rice

8 cardamom pods

500 ml/16 fl oz milk

50 g/1¾ oz/¼ cup sugar

1 strip of orange zest

4 tbsp honey

2 tbsp water

juice of 2 oranges

100 ml/3½ fl oz double (heavy) cream

Put the rice in a saucepan, cover with cold water and bring to the boil. Drain and rinse under cold water.

Coarsely grind the cardamom pods in a spice mill or coffee grinder. Discard the pieces of pod.

Combine the milk, sugar and orange zest in a heavy saucepan. Add half of the cardamom. Bring to the boil, stirring to dissolve the sugar. Stir in the rice. Reduce the heat to low, cover the pan and leave to cook very gently – just simmering – for 1 hour, stirring from time to time.

Meanwhile, put the honey, water, orange juice and remaining cardamom in a small saucepan. Bring to the boil and boil to reduce to a thick syrup. Pass through a fine sieve, then leave to cool completely.

When the rice is cooked, remove from the heat and leave to cool with the lid on. When completely cold, stir in the cream.

Spoon the creamy rice into soup bowls and top with the syrup.

Bruno's note

● I prefer rice pudding cold and very creamy. I know this is unusual, but try it and judge for yourself!

Steamed Lemon Pudding

Pudding au Citron à la Vapeur

Puddings, like other great British institutions, are not the French cup of tea. But I have learned to appreciate puddings, and over the years have developed my own versions of traditional ones.

Here, by whisking the eggs until they are thick and increased n volume, the finished pudding is lighter but still has a rich flavour. Instead of jam you can spoon lemon syrup over the puddings.

---

100 g/$3\frac{1}{2}$ oz/$\frac{1}{2}$ cup caster (granulated) sugar

2 eggs

125 g/$4\frac{1}{3}$ oz/$8\frac{1}{2}$ tbsp soft butter

125 g/$4\frac{1}{3}$ oz/$\frac{3}{4}$ cup + 2 tbsp self-raising (self-rising) flour

pinch of baking powder

grated zest and juice of 1 lemon

strawberry jam or preserves

crème fraîche

4 servings

Well butter 4 dariole moulds or custard cups and put them in the refrigerator.

Combine the sugar and eggs in a heatproof bowl. Set over a pan of simmering water and whisk energetically (or beat with a hand-held electric mixer) until the mixture is white and fluffy and will make a ribbon trail on itself when the whisk is lifted out. Remove the bowl from over the pan of water and keep whisking until the mixture is cool.

Add the soft butter and whisk well to mix, then whisk in the flour, baking powder and lemon zest and juice, mixing well. Put the lemon mixture in a piping (pastry) bag fitted with a large plain nozzle.

Preheat the oven to 150°C/300°F/Gas 3.

Butter the moulds again. Pipe the lemon mixture into the moulds to fill them to about two-thirds. Cover each mould with a disc of buttered grease-proof (wax) paper or baking parchment, then cover tightly with a lid of foil.

Set the moulds in a small roasting pan and pour enough boiling water into the pan to come halfway up the sides of the moulds. Cover the pan with foil, then place it in the oven. Cook for about 50 minutes.

To serve, unmould each pudding on to the centre of a dessert plate. Spoon some strawberry jam on top and pour a bit of crème fraîche around.

Bruno's note   ● If you prefer, you can steam the puddings on top of the stove. The water in the roasting pan should be kept at a low simmer.

Waffles and Jam

Gaufres à la Confiture

I have never found an equal to my grandmother's waffles. What was her secret? I've tried many different recipes, but have never managed to duplicate hers. The recipe here is the closest I can get. For a real treat, have only these for dinner, with jam and cream or ice cream!

Makes about 16

50 g/1⅔ oz/3½ tbsp butter

270 g/9½ oz/just under 2 cups plain (all-purpose) flour

50 g/1⅔ oz/¼ cup sugar

4 pinches of salt

3 eggs, separated

350 ml/12 fl oz milk

1 tbsp rum

2 tsp orange flower water

1 tsp vanilla essence (extract)

jam to serve

Melt the butter in a small pan, then continue heating until the butter turns a light brown (*noisette*). Remove from the heat and set aside.

Combine the flour, sugar and salt in a bowl and make a well in the centre. Mix the egg yolks with the milk. Gradually pour into the well, mixing with a whisk to incorporate the flour with the liquid. When all the liquid has been added and the batter is smooth, mix in the *noisette* butter, rum, orange flower water and vanilla essence. The batter should be the consistency of double (heavy) cream.

In a separate bowl, whisk the egg whites with a pinch of salt until stiff peaks can be formed. Whisk a spoonful of the whites into the batter, then fold in the remainder using a wooden spatula.

Heat the waffle iron. Add a ladleful of batter, close the iron and leave to cook. Check after 3 minutes: the waffle should be golden brown, crisp and set.

Serve hot with jam and with cream or vanilla ice cream.

● For a more elaborate dish, top the waffles with raspberries, cover with piped meringue (flavoured with lemon zest) and bake in a hot oven for a few minutes. A sorbet would be a perfect addition to this.

Bruno's note

Crêpes

If you want the children away from the TV screen on late Sunday afternoon, then this is the way to entice them. All children seem to love crêpes, or pancakes, with jam, sugar, melted chocolate, maple syrup or whatever. The best thing about making crêpes is that everybody wants to be involved, so it can be a lot of fun!

---

140 g/5 oz/1 cup plain (all-purpose) flour	a pinch of salt	**Makes**
2 eggs	a drop of vanilla essence (extract)	**about 16**
grated zest of $\frac{1}{4}$ lemon	350 ml/12 fl oz milk	
35 g/1$\frac{1}{4}$ oz/3 tbsp caster (granulated) sugar	20 g/$\frac{2}{3}$ oz/4 tsp butter	
	vegetable oil	

Put the flour in a large mixing bowl and make a well in the centre. Put the eggs, lemon zest, sugar, salt and vanilla essence in the well and mix together with a whisk. Gradually add the milk to the egg mixture in a thin stream, whisking and incorporating the flour little by little. When all the flour is incorporated and the mixture is moist enough, whisk energetically until smooth, then finish with the rest of the milk.

Melt the butter in a small pan then continue heating until the butter turns brown (*noisette*). Stir into the batter.

Very lightly oil a 20 cm/8 inch frying pan and heat it. Pour a ladleful of batter into the pan; at the same time, tilt and rotate the pan so that the batter spreads to cover the bottom of the pan in a uniform thin layer. Cook until the base of the crêpe is set and lightly golden, then turn it over (or flip it in the air) and cook the other side just to colour it lightly. Tip the crêpe on to a plate, and make the next one.

Serve hot, with sugar, jam, maple syrup, etc.

Light Lemon and Blackcurrant Gratin

Gratin de Cassis au Citron

---

4 servings

250 g/9 oz blackcurrants (weight without stalks)

3 tbsp granulated sugar

light brown sugar to finish

$3\frac{1}{2}$ tbsp lemon juice, boiled and cooled

$\frac{1}{2}$ gelatine leaf

grated zest of 1 lemon

FOR THE CRÈME PÂTISSIÈRE

200 ml/7 fl oz milk

3 egg yolks

30 g/1 oz/$2\frac{1}{2}$ tbsp caster (granulated) sugar

25 g/$1\frac{3}{4}$ oz/3 tbsp cornflour (cornstarch)

FOR THE MERINGUE ITALIENNE

120 g/4 oz/$\frac{1}{2}$ cup + 2 tbsp sugar

2 tbsp water

10 g/$\frac{1}{3}$ oz/$\frac{1}{2}$ tbsp liquid glucose (light corn syrup)

2 egg whites

Combine the blackcurrants and granulated sugar in a saucepan and stew over a low heat, stirring occasionally, until reduced to a thick jam-like consistency. Remove from the heat and set aside.

To make the *crème pâtissière*, heat the milk in a heavy saucepan until boiling. Whisk the egg yolks with the sugar until the mixture turns white. Add the cornflour, then add the hot milk and lemon juice and mix well. Pour back into the saucepan and simmer for 5 minutes, stirring well. Remove from the heat and leave to cool a bit. Soak the gelatine in cold water until softened, then squeeze dry and add to the *crème*. Stir well. Set aside.

To make the *meringue italienne*, put the sugar, water and glucose in a saucepan and bring to the boil, stirring to dissolve the sugar. Boil for 2 minutes, then check the temperature of the syrup. Use a sugar thermometer (you should be at the soft ball stage) or your fingers: dip two fingers into a small bowl of cold water, dip quickly into the syrup and then immediately dip again into the cold water. You should be able to form the syrup into a ball between your fingers. As soon as the syrup has reached the correct temperature, remove the pan from the heat. Whisk the egg whites in a bowl using an electric mixer. When the whites are stiff, gradually whisk in the sugar syrup. Continue whisking until the meringue is completely cooled.

Fold the meringue into the *crème pâtissière* using a rubber spatula. Fold in the lemon zest.

Preheat the oven to 160°C/325°F/Gas 3.

Put 2 spoonfuls of the lemon cream into each of 4 buttered individual gratin dishes. Divide the blackcurrant 'jam' among the dishes and top with the rest of the lemon cream. Smooth the top. Sprinkle with an even layer of brown sugar and melt and colour with a blow torch or under the grill (broiler). Place the dishes in the oven and heat for 6–8 minutes. Serve immediately.

● This recipe will work quite well with orange and grapefruit segments or some fresh raspberries.   **Bruno's note**

Prunes Four Quarters

Quatre Quarts

Like me, my mother didn't have a sweet tooth, and cake-making was one of her nightmares. But one of the cakes she *did* like to make was the simplest you can imagine, the 'Quatre Quarts'.

It's made with a quarter of flour, a quarter of sugar, a quarter of butter and a quarter of eggs. Mix it, bake and it's ready. So easy!

Makes a loaf cake

250 g/9 oz/1 cup + 2 tbsp soft butter

250 g/9 oz/1¼ cups caster (granulated) sugar

250 g/9 oz eggs (4)

grated zest of 1 orange

200 g/7 oz/1¼ cups plain (all-purpose) flour

50 g/1⅔ oz/6½ tbsp cornflour (cornstarch)

2 tsp baking powder

250 g/9 oz pitted prunes

TO SERVE

sweetened plain yogurt

Armagnac or rum

Preheat the oven to 220°C/425°F/Gas 7. Butter and flour a 1.3–1.5 litre/2¼–2½ pint/1¼–1½ quart capacity loaf pan and line the bottom and sides with greaseproof (wax) paper.

Put the butter and sugar in a mixing bowl and beat together until smooth and white. Add the eggs, one at a time, beating well between each addition. When all the eggs have been incorporated, add the orange zest, flour, cornflour and baking powder. Mix just to blend the ingredients evenly, but don't overdo it.

Turn the cake mixture into the prepared pan and arrange the prunes over the top. Bake for 10 minutes, then reduce the oven temperature to 170°C/325°F/Gas 3 and bake for a further 40 minutes or until a skewer inserted into the centre comes out clean.

When the cake is cooked, turn it out on to a wire rack to cool.

Serve the cake sliced, with sweetened yogurt flavoured with Armagnac or rum.

Lemon Verbena Crème Brûlée

Crème Brûlée à la Verveine

6 egg yolks

40 g/1$\frac{1}{2}$ oz/3 tbsp sugar

500 ml/16 fl oz double (heavy)
  cream

grated zest of 1 lemon

15 lemon verbena or lemon balm
  leaves

1 tbsp Strega liqueur (optional)

demerara or light brown sugar to
  finish

4 servings

Preheat the oven to 180°C/350°F/Gas 4.

Combine the egg yolks and sugar in a bowl and mix well together.

Put the cream into a heavy saucepan and add the lemon zest and leaves. Bring to the boil, then pour the cream over the egg yolk mixture, whisking energetically. Pour the mixture back into the pan and stir over a low heat until the custard thickens enough to coat the back of the spoon.

Pass the custard through a fine sieve. Stir in the Strega if using. Divide the custard among 4 ramekins, each 7.5 cm/3 inch diameter and 150 ml/5 fl oz capacity. Place a layer of newspaper on the bottom of a small roasting pan and set the ramekins on top. Add enough warm water to the pan to come three-quarters of the way up the sides of the ramekins. Place in the oven and bake for about 20 minutes or until the custards are just set. Shake gently: if they are still runny in the middle leave them in the oven for a few more minutes.

When cooked, remove from the oven and leave to cool completely. If you have made them in advance, store them in the refrigerator and take them out about 30 minutes before serving.

Preheat the grill (broiler).

Sprinkle the top of each cream with a layer of brown sugar and melt and glaze this quickly under the grill or by using a blow torch. Leave to cool to room temperature before serving.

- When cooking the custard on top of the stove, if it gets a bit too hot and starts to curdle, pour it quickly into the blender or food processor and blend. It will become smooth again.

- If you want more of the crisp sugar top, use a gratin dish instead of individual ramekins.

Floating Islands with Pernod

Iles Flottante au Pernod

4–6 servings

1 litre/1⅔ pints/1 quart milk

2 strips of pared orange zest

1 vanilla pod (bean), split in half
    lengthways

12 egg yolks

120 g/4 oz/½ cup + 2 tbsp caster
    (granulated) sugar

3 tbsp Pernod

FOR THE MERINGUE

6 egg whites

a pinch of salt

100 g/3½ oz/½ cup caster (superfine)
    sugar

TO FINISH

100 g/3½ oz/½ cup caster
    (granulated) sugar

toasted flaked (sliced) almonds

Put the milk in a heavy saucepan with the orange zest and vanilla. Bring to the boil.

Meanwhile, in a mixing bowl, beat the egg yolks with the sugar until thick and white. Pour the hot milk into the egg yolk mixture, whisking well, then pour the mixture back into the saucepan. Cook over low heat, stirring constantly with a wooden spoon, until the cream thickens enough to coat the spoon. Do not boil.

Pass the cream through a fine sieve into a bowl. Leave to cool completely, then cover and refrigerate.

To make the meringue, put the egg whites and a tiny pinch of salt in a large clean stainless steel or glass bowl and whisk to a soft peak. Gradually add the sugar and continue whisking until the meringue is stiff.

With two large spoons dipped in hot water, shape the meringue into 8 *quenelles* and place on a plate, arranging them so they are not touching each other. Cook in the microwave on High for 15 seconds, rotating them if you don't have a turntable. Leave to cool.

Flavour the cream with the Pernod and pour into a large serving dish. Top with the soft meringue *quenelles*.

To finish, melt the sugar in a saucepan and cook it to a caramel. Drizzle it over the meringues. Sprinkle with some toasted flaked almonds.

- The classic method for making *Iles Flottante* is to infuse the warm milk with the flavourings for 20 minutes and then to cook the meringue *quenelles* in the simmering milk for 2 minutes on each side. The meringue are then left to drain on a wet cloth while you continue with the making of the cream. You can, of course, use this method rather than the quick microwave method given here. To turn the meringues in the poaching milk, push down on one side; they will then roll over. If you try to turn them by scooping them with a spoon, you'll find you are chasing them all over the pan while they bob around.

- To check the colour of the caramel, dip in a slip of white paper. When the caramel is the right colour, dip the base of the pan in cold water and stir the caramel gently to stop further cooking. Then dry the pan before pouring the caramel over the meringues.

- If you don't like Pernod, other flavourings can be used, such as Grand Marnier, pistachio or praline.

Lightly Poached Strawberries with Green Peppercorn Ice Cream

Fraises Pochées, Glace au Poivre Vert

The Italians have a dish of strawberries with balsamic vinegar and freshly ground black pepper. It must be said that this is quite unusual! But it is surprising how well the peppercorns go with the strawberries. I love strawberries and cream, so I thought what about combining those flavours with the peppery ones? The result is a creamy and delectable dessert.

---

4 servings

900 g/2 lb strawberries

500 ml/16 fl oz water

200 g/7 oz/1 cup sugar

400 ml/14 fl oz *crème anglaise* (page 214)

2 tsp (8 g) green peppercorns in brine, drained and dried

1 tsp liquid glucose (light corn syrup)

sprigs of fresh mint to decorate

Put 250 g/9 oz of the strawberries in the blender or food processor and blend until smooth. Press through a sieve. Set this coulis aside.

Combine the water and sugar in a saucepan and heat, stirring to dissolve the sugar. Bring to the boil and boil for 2 minutes, then pour the syrup into a bowl. Add the remaining strawberries and the strawberry coulis and stir gently to mix. Set a plate on top to be sure the strawberries are completely immersed in the syrup, then leave to cool. When cold, refrigerate.

Put the *crème anglaise* into a blender and add the green peppercorns and glucose. Process until smooth. Alternatively, you can use a hand blender. Pour into an ice cream machine and freeze.

With a slotted spoon, remove the strawberries from the syrup to a clean bowl. Strain the syrup over the berries.

To serve, divide the strawberries and syrup among glass cups or soup bowls. Top each serving with a ball of ice cream and add a sprig of mint.

Bruno's note

● If you prefer the fruit to be uncooked, marinate the strawberries with a squeeze of lemon, a little sugar and a dash of Grand Marnier.

Cherry Beer Ice Cream

Glace à la Krick

In 1992 I was asked to prepare a buffet (hot and cold) for the launch of a new beer. The beer was Belgian, so the food needed to be appropriate. Having worked in Belgium, I remembered an interesting beer flavoured with cherry, called Krick. I decided to use it in a dessert, where the flavour of the beer could be appreciated, and came up with this simple ice cream.

---

1 can of black cherries in syrup

330 ml/11 fl oz cherry beer, plus a little extra for serving

500 ml/16 fl oz milk

6 egg yolks

1 tbsp liquid glucose (light corn syrup)

120 ml/4 fl oz soured cream

6 servings

Put the syrup from the can of cherries and the beer in a large, fairly wide pan. Bring to the boil and boil until reduced by three-quarters. Set aside.

Bring the milk to the boil in a heavy-based saucepan. Mix the eggs yolks together in a bowl. Gradually pour in the hot milk, mixing well, then stir in the glucose. Pour the mixture back into the saucepan and cook over low heat, stirring, until the custard thickens enough to coat the spoon. Pour the custard through a fine sieve into a bowl. Stir in the reduced syrup and beer mixture. Roughly chop the cherries and stir in. When the mixture is cold, stir in the soured cream.

Pour into an ice cream machine and freeze. When the ice cream is set, spoon it into a plastic container and place in the freezer. The ice cream can be kept for 1–2 days.

To serve, scoop the ice cream into balls and put in dessert glasses. Pour a bit of cherry beer over the ice cream, in front of your guests. Serve with crisp sweet biscuits (cookies).

● To enhance the cherry flavour, you can add 3 tablespoons of kirsch before freezing the ice cream. **Bruno's note**

Rice Pudding Ice Cream with Fruit Compote

Glace de Riz au Lait, Compote de Fruits

4 servings

1 litre/1$\frac{2}{3}$ pints/1 quart milk

1 vanilla pod (bean)

2 large strips of dried orange zest

80 g/scant 3 oz/6$\frac{1}{2}$ tbsp sugar

80 g/ scant 3 oz/6$\frac{1}{2}$ tbsp short-grain
    pudding rice

2 tsp liquid glucose (light corn
    syrup)

fresh mint leaves to finish

FOR THE FRUIT COMPOTE

200 g/7 oz/1 cup sugar

600 ml/1 pint/2$\frac{1}{2}$ cups water

1 pear

4 peaches

1 grapefruit

1 punnet of raspberries

Combine the milk, vanilla pod, orange zest and sugar in a heavy saucepan. Bring to the boil, stirring to dissolve the sugar, then add the rice. Lower the heat so the liquid is just simmering, cover with a lid and leave to cook for 1 hour.

Drain the rice in a colander set in a bowl. Set the rice aside. Pour the milk back into the saucepan and boil to reduce to the consistency of *crème anglaise*. Stir in the glucose. Leave to cool.

Discard the vanilla pod and orange zest from the rice. Set aside one third of the cooked rice for another dish. Add the remaining rice to the reduced milk. Churn in an ice cream machine until frozen. Transfer the rice pudding ice cream to a suitable freezer container and keep in the freezer until serving.

To make the fruit compote, dissolve the sugar in the water in a saucepan and boil for 5 minutes. Meanwhile, peel the pear, quarter it and cut out the core. Peel the peaches, cut them in half and remove the stones; reserve the stones. Cut each peach half in half. Peel and segment the grapefruit. Add the pear quarters to the sugar syrup and simmer until just tender when pierced with a knife blade. Add the peach quarters with the stones and simmer gently for 5 minutes. Finally, stir in the grapefruit and raspberries. Remove from the heat, cover and leave to cool completely.

Before serving, let the ice cream soften a bit at room temperature. Spoon the fruit compote into the bottom of serving glasses or soup plates. Add two *quenelle* shapes or round scoops of ice cream on top and garnish with mint leaves.

Bruno's notes

- Look for liquid glucose in a chemist's. If there is none in stock they can probably order it for you. The glucose prevents the formation of ice crystals, so the ice cream has a smooth, homogeneous texture.

- The reason for cooking more rice than is used is that you need the starch from a larger quantity of rice to give creaminess to the ice cream. Although you discard (or eat) some of the rice, by making this ice cream you save 6 egg yolks!

- This ice cream will keep very well in the freezer.

- You can turn the unused rice into a little tart: whisk an egg white with caster sugar to make a meringue, fold in the rice and put into a baked pastry case. Bake in a hot oven for about 5 minutes. Serve with a fruit coulis.

Figs Carpaccio with Red Wine Granité

Carpaccio de Figue, Granité au Vin Rouge

This is a delicious dessert that is incredibly easy to make.

4 servings

2 tbsp honey

2 tbsp water

juice of $\frac{1}{2}$ lemon

$\frac{1}{2}$ tsp ground fennel seeds

12 nice purple figs

sprigs of fresh mint to decorate

FOR THE GRANITÉ

250 ml/8 fl oz fruity red wine

150 ml/5 fl oz water

80 g/scant 3 oz/6 tbsp sugar

6 black peppercorns, crushed with the side of a knife

$\frac{1}{2}$ bay leaf

First make the *granité*. Combine all the ingredients in a saucepan and heat, stirring, to dissolve the sugar. Bring to the boil, then cover and remove from the heat. When the mixture is cool, pass it through a fine sieve into a small metal tray. Place in the freezer. When the surface of the mixture starts to set, mix it into the unfrozen mixture using a fork. Leave to freeze for another 10 minutes, then repeat the mixing. Continue doing this to obtain a granular texture.

Put the honey, water, lemon juice and fennel seeds in a small saucepan and bring to the boil. Cover, remove from the heat and leave to cool completely.

When ready to serve, slice the figs thinly and arrange them on the plates. Brush the fennel and honey syrup all over the fig slices, then leave to marinate for 15 minutes.

Spoon the *granité* into the centre of each plate, add a mint sprig and serve.

Jasmin Tea and Lemon Parfait

Parfait de Thé au Jasmin et Citron

150 g/5 oz/$\frac{3}{4}$ cup sugar

100 ml/$3\frac{1}{2}$ fl oz water

1 tbsp jasmin tea leaves

6 egg yolks

2 tbsp lemon juice

450 ml/15 fl oz whipping cream, whipped until thick

grated zest of 1 lemon

canned lychees in syrup to serve

fresh mint leaves to decorate

10 servings

Combine the sugar and water in a saucepan and bring to the boil, stirring to dissolve the sugar. Add the tea leaves and stir, then cover and remove from the heat. Leave to steep for 5 minutes. Strain the syrup through a fine sieve into a clean pan and bring back to the boil.

Put the egg yolks in a large bowl. Pour in the boiling syrup in a thin stream, beating well. Then slowly pour in the lemon juice and continue beating until the mixture becomes white and fluffy. Beat until completely cool. Chill for 5 minutes.

Fold the whipped cream and lemon zest into the mixture. Pour into a 25 x 10 cm/10 x 4 inch terrine mould or loaf pan lined with cling film (plastic wrap). Cover and freeze until set.

To serve, cut 2 cm/$\frac{3}{4}$ inch slices of *parfait* and place in the centre of each plate. Garnish with a few lychees and mint leaves.

● This *parfait* will keep very well for a week or so in the freezer.

Bruno's note

Apple Tart

Tarte aux Pommes

---

6 servings

1 kg/2¼ lb cooking apples

50 g/1⅔ oz/3½ tbsp butter

¼ tsp ground cinnamon

50 g/1⅔ oz/¼ cup sugar

5 Granny Smith's or Cox's
  apples

melted butter

sifted icing (confectioners')
  sugar

apricot jam

FOR THE PASTRY

200 g/7 oz/1¼ cups plain (all-
  purpose) flour

1 egg

1 tbsp cold water

a pinch of salt

2 pinches of baking powder

100 g/3½ oz/7 tbsp soft unsalted
  butter

½ tsp vanilla essence (extract)

1 egg yolk lightly beaten with 1 tsp
  water, to glaze

First make the pastry dough. Sift the flour on to the work surface in a pile and make a well in the centre. Put the remaining pastry ingredients (except the egg glaze) into the well and blend them together with your fingertips. Gradually work in the flour to make a dough that will hold together. Mix and knead the dough by pushing it away from you on the surface with the heel of your hand. When the dough is smooth and will peel easily from the work surface, shape it into a ball, wrap and chill for 30 minutes.

Meanwhile, peel and core the cooking apples and chop them coarsely. Melt the butter with the cinnamon in a large heavy saucepan. Add the chopped apples and sugar and stir to mix. Leave to simmer gently until pulped, stirring occasionally, then continue cooking to evaporate excess liquid, leaving a thick apple compote. Remove from the heat and set aside.

Preheat the oven to 200°C/400°F/Gas 6.

Roll out the pastry dough and use to line a 23 cm/9 inch loose-bottomed

STUFFED TOMATO OLD-FASHIONED STYLE, *PAGE 132*, **WITH PEAS FRENCH-STYLE,** *PAGE 143*

RICE PUDDING ICE CREAM WITH FRUIT COMPOTE, *PAGE 174*

flan or tart mould. Roll the rolling pin over the top of the mould to cut off excess dough. Press the dough firmly against the side of the mould to make the sides of the pastry case thinner and so they rise about 3 mm/$\frac{1}{8}$ inch above the rim of the mould. With your fingertips, gently pinch and twist this top edge to flute it. Prick the bottom of the pastry case all over with a fork, then line with greaseproof (wax) paper. Fill with baking beans. Chill for 10 minutes.

Bake the pastry case for 10 minutes, then carefully remove the paper and beans. Brush the pastry case with the egg glaze and bake for a further 5 minutes. Remove from the oven and fill with the apple compote, smoothing the surface.

Peel and core the Granny Smith's and slice them finely. Arrange neatly over the apple compote, overlapping the slices slightly in concentric rings. Brush the apple slices with melted butter and dust with icing sugar. Return to the oven and bake for 25 minutes.

Glaze the top of the tart with melted and sieved apricot jam, then leave the tart to cool in the mould.

● You could serve this with crème fraîche or vanilla ice cream.   **Bruno's note**

Chocolate Tartlet with Coffee Cream

Tartelette au Chocolat Sauce Café

This is definitely a dessert for chocolate lovers! When perfectly cooked, the soft chocolate filling in the crisp tartlet shell is a wicked surprise!

4 servings

100 g/3½ oz bitter chocolate

2 eggs

30 g/1 oz caster (granulated) sugar

30 g/1 oz/2 tbsp unsalted butter, melted and cooled

½ tsp unsweetened cocoa powder

½ tsp cornflour (cornstarch)

grated zest of ⅓ orange

icing (confectioners') sugar to finish

FOR THE SHORTBREAD

150 g/5 oz/1 cup plain (all-purpose) flour

100 g/3½ oz/7 tbsp soft unsalted butter

a pinch of salt

75 g/2½ oz/9½ tbsp icing (confectioners') sugar, sifted

1 egg

FOR THE COFFEE CREAM

1 tbsp instant coffee mixed with 3 tbsp hot water

200 ml/7 fl oz *crème anglaise* (page 214)

First make the shortbread dough. Sift the flour on to the work surface in a pile and make a well in the centre. Put the butter, salt and sugar into the well and mix together with your fingertips. Gradually work in the flour. Use the heel of your hand to spread out the mixture and then crumble it between your hands. When the ingredients are thoroughly combined, mix in the egg to bind to a dough. Shape into a ball, wrap and chill for at least 2 hours.

Preheat the oven to 180°C/350°F/Gas 4.

Roll out the dough to about 3 mm/⅛ inch thick and cut out 4 discs, each 10–11 cm/4–4½ inches in diameter. Line four 8 cm/3¼ inch tartlet moulds with the discs. Press foil smoothly into the tartlet cases and fill with baking beans. Bake for 10 minutes or until the pastry is just set. Carefully remove the foil and beans, then bake for a further 2 minutes. Set the tartlet cases aside to cool.

Melt the chocolate in a small bowl placed over a pan of simmering water. Set aside. Put the eggs in a large bowl and add the caster sugar. Set the bowl over the pan of simmering water and whisk energetically until the mixture is very thick and pale and it will make a ribbon trail on itself when the whisk is lifted out. Add the melted chocolate, melted butter and cocoa powder, whisking well, then finish with the cornflour and orange zest.

Fill the tartlet cases with the chocolate mixture. Bake in the preheated oven for 6–8 minutes or until the filling is slightly risen.

Meanwhile, mix the coffee with the *crème anglaise*.

To serve, spoon the coffee cream on to the plates and tilt and rotate to spread out the cream evenly. Set a tartlet in the middle of each plate and dust the top with icing sugar.

● When cooked, the filling will not be completely set in the middle, but should still move a little when shaken.   **Bruno's note**

Vanilla Profiteroles
with Chocolate Sauce

Profiteroles au Chocolat

When I was a boy, my parents used to take us to a small village restaurant where you could eat for 45 francs (about £5). There was no choice, and everyone sat together at a large table. The greatest treat was when profiteroles were on the menu. My daughter loves these scrumptious buns filled with vanilla ice cream and covered with warm chocolate sauce – and so do I!

8 servings

10 g/$\frac{1}{3}$ oz/scant 1 tbsp sugar

100 g/$3\frac{1}{2}$ oz/7 tbsp soft butter, cut into small pieces

pinch of salt

500 ml/16 fl oz water

150 g/5 oz/1 cup self-raising (self-rising) flour

4–5 eggs

1 egg yolk beaten with 2 tsp water

vanilla ice cream

warm chocolate sauce (page 213)

Preheat the oven to 250°C/500°F/Gas 10.

Combine the sugar, butter, salt and water in a heavy saucepan. Bring to the boil, stirring to dissolve the sugar and melt the butter. As soon as the water is boiling, remove the pan from the heat and quickly add the flour. Mix energetically with a wooden spoon until the mixture stops sticking to the pan and the spoon. Turn the mixture into a bowl. Add the eggs one at a time, beating well. Make sure each is well absorbed before adding the next. The mixture should become smooth and shiny with no trace of fat – you may not need to add all of the last egg.

Put the mixture into a piping (pastry) bag fitted with a 1.5–2 cm/$\frac{1}{2}$–$\frac{3}{4}$ inch plain nozzle. Pipe in 40 little blobs on a lightly buttered baking sheet. Brush with the egg yolk wash and lightly mark a criss-cross on top of each with the back of a fork. Bake for 10 minutes, then reduce the oven temperature to 220°C/425°F/Gas 7 and open the oven door slightly. Continue baking with the door slightly ajar for 15 minutes or until the buns are nicely coloured and dry. When tapped on the base they should sound hollow. Cool on a wire rack.

Let the ice cream soften slightly at room temperature, then stir it and put it into a piping (pastry) bag. Make a small hole in the base of each bun. Working quickly (so the ice cream doesn't melt completely), pipe the ice cream into the buns. Keep the buns in the freezer until 5 minutes before you are going to serve them.

To serve, arrange 5 buns on each plate and spoon the warm chocolate sauce over them.

Bruno's notes

- The butter should be completely melted when the water reaches a boil, so that the water does not continue to boil and start to evaporate.
- When piping the buns, leave at least 4 cm/1$\frac{1}{2}$ inches space between them because they will rise and spread during baking.
- Marking the tops with a criss-cross makes them even so they will have a nice shape once baked, and they won't crack.
- Leaving the oven door ajar allows the steam from the buns to escape.
- If the buns are too dry when you take them out of the oven, cover them with a cloth before leaving to cool. This will soften them a little.
- You could also fill the buns with *crème Chantilly* (sweetened whipped cream flavoured with vanilla) and dip the tops in caramel, or just dust with icing (confectioners') sugar.

Cherry Pithivier

Pithivier aux Cerises

4–5 servings

25 g/scant 1 oz/2 tbsp butter

60 g/2 oz/½ cup icing (confectioners') sugar, plus extra to dust

400 g/14 oz canned pitted sweet black cherries (drained weight)

1 tbsp kirsch

400 g/14 oz puff pastry

1 egg yolk lightly beaten with 1 tsp water

FOR THE ALMOND CREAM

60 g/2 oz/4 tbsp soft butter

30 g/1 oz/¼ cup icing (confectioners') sugar

60 g/2 oz/⅔ cup ground almonds

1 tbsp flour

1 egg

Melt the butter in a heavy saucepan. When foamy, add the sugar and cherries and stir well. Pour in the kirsch and set alight. The cherries should start to caramelize nicely. When the flames have died away, remove from the heat and set aside to cool.

To make the almond cream, put the butter in a mixing bowl and work with a spatula until very soft and creamy. Add the sugar, almonds and flour and mix very well, then add the egg. Beat until the mixture is light and thoroughly blended. Add the cold cherry mixture to the almond cream. Mix together, then cover and refrigerate.

Cut the puff pastry into two portions, one weighing 250 g/9 oz and the other 150 g/5 oz. The smaller portion will be the base, so start by rolling it out to a 20 cm/8 inch disc that is about 2 mm/less than ⅛ inch thick. Roll up around the rolling pin, then unroll on a baking sheet.

Roll out the larger portion of puff pastry to a 21 cm/8½ inch disc.

Preheat the oven to 220°C/425°F/Gas 7.

Spoon the cherry and almond mixture into the middle of the pastry base, leaving 2.5 cm/1 inch clear all around. Brush this border with the egg wash. Lay the larger pastry disc on top and smooth down gently. Press to seal to the egg-washed border. Place a 19 cm/7½ inch diameter plate on top and use a sharp knife to cut off excess pastry around it, cutting straight down; remove the plate. With the flat rounded tip of a table knife, make depressions at regular intervals all around the pastry edge to crimp it. Then hold the knife blade vertically, at a 45° angle to the edge, and make shallow cuts all around the side. Cut a little steam hole in the centre of the top. Decorate the top by scoring curved lines from the hole to the edge. Glaze the top with the egg wash.

Bake for 6 minutes, then lower the oven temperature to 200°C/400°F/ Gas 6 and bake for a further 20 minutes. Dust the top of the pithiviers with sifted icing sugar. Return to a 220°C/425°F/Gas 7 oven and bake for a few more minutes to give the top a shiny glaze. Transfer to a wire rack to cool.

Serve with vanilla ice cream or cherry beer ice cream (page 173).

Baked Apple with Mincemeat and a Puff Pastry Cap

Pomme au Four Fourrée de Fruits 'Chapeau' de Feuilletage

4 servings

4 large, firm, tart-sweet apples such
    as Cox's

200 g/7 oz mincemeat

1 tbsp Calvados or brandy

100 g/3½ oz/7 tbsp butter

4 tbsp cider (hard cider)

250 g/9 oz puff pastry

1 egg yolk lightly beaten with 1 tsp
    water

crème fraîche to serve

Make a few lengthwise cuts in the skin of each apple, to prevent them bursting during cooking. Using a melon baller or small knife, cut the core out of each apple. Start at the top and don't cut all the way through. Cut a little more apple away to make a hollow for stuffing.

Mix the mincemeat with the Calvados and half of the butter. Use to fill the hollow in the apples. Set the apples in a small baking dish and add the rest of the butter and the cider to the dish.

Preheat the oven to 200°C/400°F/Gas 6.

Roll out the puff pastry to about 3 mm/⅛ inch thick and cut out 4 discs, each 10 cm/4 inches in diameter. Brush the discs with egg wash on one side and place on the apples, egg-washed side down. Smooth down over the apples and seal well to the sides. Brush the top of the discs with egg wash.

Bake for 10 minutes, then reduce the oven temperature to 160°C/325°F/ Gas 3 and bake for a further 10 minutes or until the apples are just tender and the pastry is golden.

Serve hot, with the cooking juices and crème fraîche.

Sweet Pastry Fritters

Bugnes Lyonnaise

These fritters, called *bugnes* in France, are enjoyed by the young and also by the not so young. I'm not sure about their origin, although Lyon is most associated with them. Most grandmothers in France always seem to have a tin of differently shaped *bugnes* in their kitchen. The fritters are good simply as a treat in the afternoon, but they can also be served as a dessert with jam or to accompany a *crème brûlée*, for example.

---

170 g/6 oz/$1\frac{1}{4}$ cups plain (all-purpose) flour

1 tsp baking powder

2 pinches of salt

60 g/2 oz/5 tbsp caster (granulated) sugar

2 egg yolks

70 g/$2\frac{1}{2}$ oz/5 tbsp soft unsalted butter

grated zest of $\frac{1}{2}$ lemon

2 tbsp rum

vegetable oil for frying

Makes about 20

Pile the flour on the work surface and make a well in the centre. Put the remaining ingredients into the well and mix together with your fingertips. Gradually work in the flour and knead to a smooth dough. Do not overwork the dough.

Roll out the dough on a lightly floured surface to 3 mm/$\frac{1}{8}$ inch thick. Cut out rectangles that are 12 cm/5 inches long and 5 cm/2 inches wide. Make a slit down the centre of each rectangle and push through one end to make a loose knot shape.

Heat a pan of oil to 160–170°C/about 325°F. Fry the fritters in batches until they are puffed and golden on both sides. Drain on paper towels and leave to cool. Sprinkle with vanilla sugar or caster sugar before serving.

● These can be kept in an airtight tin, lined with paper towels, for 3–4 days.

Bruno's note

Coconut and Chocolate Macaroon

Macaron au Coco et Chocolat

---

4 servings

2 oranges

Grand Marnier

icing (confectioners') sugar and
    sprigs of fresh mint to decorate

FOR THE MACAROONS

2 egg whites

$\frac{1}{2}$ teaspoon vanilla essence (extract)

a pinch of salt

80 g/scant 3 oz/6$\frac{1}{2}$ tbsp caster
    (superfine) sugar

2 tbsp flour

130 g/4$\frac{1}{2}$ oz/1$\frac{1}{3}$ cups desiccated
    (dried shredded) coconut

FOR THE GANACHE FILLING

70 ml/2$\frac{1}{2}$ fl oz/5 tbsp double (heavy)
    cream

120 g/4 oz dark chocolate, broken
    into small pieces

60 g/2 oz/4 tbsp soft unsalted butter

grated zest of $\frac{1}{2}$ orange

2 tsp Grand Marnier

First make the macaroons. Preheat the oven to 180°C/350°F/Gas 4. Line one or two baking sheets with greaseproof (wax) paper.

In a mixing bowl, whisk the egg whites until foamy. Add the vanilla and salt and continue beating until the whites will form soft peaks. Slowly beat in the sugar and beat until the whites will form stiff peaks. Add the flour and coconut and fold in gently with a rubber spatula.

Put the coconut meringue into a piping (pastry) bag and pipe on to the prepared baking sheets in 8 mounds that are about 4 cm/1$\frac{1}{2}$ inches in diameter. Leave about 5 cm/2 inches of space between each mound, to allow for spreading.

Leave at room temperature for about 15 minutes or until a thin crust forms on top of the mounds, then bake in the preheated oven, with the door slightly ajar to avoid any steam, for about 8 minutes or until crusty on the outside but still soft within. Transfer the macaroons to a wire rack and leave to cool.

Peel the oranges, removing all the white pith, and cut out the segments. Sprinkle the orange segments with a little Grand Marnier and set aside.

To make the filling, put the cream in a small saucepan and bring to the boil. Remove from the heat. Add the chocolate and stir until melted, then whisk energetically. When the mixture starts to thicken, add the soft butter, orange zest and Grand Marnier. Set the base of the pan in a container of iced water and whisk until the chocolate *ganache* is thick.

Use a palette knife (metal spatula) to spread the *ganache* over the bases of four of the macaroons. Stick the other macaroons on top, base to base.

Arrange the orange segments in the centre of the plates and set a 'macaroon' sandwich on top. Dust with icing sugar and finish with a sprig of mint.

● You can make the macaroons the day before. They will keep well in an airtight tin. **Bruno's note**

Fennel Seed Brioche

Brioche aux Graines de Fenouil

Amongst pastry chefs, brioche is known as 'the lady', and is much respected. Only the best ingredients will do: top quality butter and the freshest eggs. Brioche does take time, and you may need to make several attempts before a perfect result is achieved, but I guarantee it is worth all the effort. When you cut the brioche you will savour the most wonderful sweet smell of butter and yeast. A very special treat with a cup of coffee on Sunday afternoon.

Makes

1 large brioche

10 g/$\frac{1}{3}$ oz fresh yeast

2 tbsp lukewarm milk

250 g/8 oz/1$\frac{2}{3}$ cups strong white (white bread) flour

25 g/1 oz/2 tbsp sugar

5 g/scant 1 tsp salt

3 eggs

125 g/4 oz/$\frac{1}{2}$ cup soft butter

1 tsp ground fennel seeds

1 egg yolk lightly beaten with 2 tsp water

demerara (raw brown) sugar

Put the yeast and lukewarm milk in a large mixing bowl and mix with a whisk to dissolve the yeast. Add the flour, sugar, salt and 2 eggs to the bowl. With your hands, mix the ingredients together to make a firm dough. Turn the dough on to the work surface and knead until the dough is smooth and no longer sticky and has some elasticity.

Return the dough to the bowl and add the remaining egg. Using your fingers, pinch and squeeze the dough and egg together until combined – this will take a bit of time. The resulting dough will be smooth and shiny and should be quite elastic.

Gradually work in the soft butter, mixing it into the dough bit by bit with your fingers. Then pull the dough together into a ball and sprinkle the fennel on top. Cover the bowl with a cloth and set aside in a warm place (25–30°C/77–86°F) for 1 hour or until the dough has doubled in volume.

Punch the dough with your fist to knock out the air, then press together. Shape into a ball again. Cover the bowl with a cloth and put into the refrigerator. Leave for 3 hours. After this time, the dough should have risen again to twice the volume.

Punch down the dough once again, then turn it on to a lightly floured marble slab or other cold work surface. Press it out to flatten it, then fold in the sides and press together. Shape it into a smooth ball and place in a fluted mould: the dough should half fill the mould. Leave to rise in a warm place again until doubled in size.

Preheat the oven to 180°C/350°F/Gas 4.

Brush the top of the brioche with the egg yolk glaze and sprinkle lightly with demerara sugar. Bake for about 40 minutes or until risen and golden brown. A skewer inserted into the centre should come out dry. Turn out on to a wire rack to cool.

- For the best result, I suggest you use an electronic scale to measure the ingredients. **Bruno's notes**
- If you have an electric mixer with a dough hook, you can use this for kneading instead of doing it by hand.
- Use this to make brioche and butter pudding.

BASIC RECIPES

White Chicken stock

Fond de Volaille

Makes 2.25 litres/4¼ pints/ 2 quarts

2 kg/4½ lb chicken carcasses, wings and bones

200 g/7 oz celery, chopped

200 g/7 oz onions, chopped

200 g/7 oz leeks, chopped

3 garlic cloves, crushed with the side of a knife

1 sprig of fresh thyme

1 bay leaf

a few parsley stalks

pinch of salt

Put the cut up chicken carcasses, wings and chicken bones in a large pot. Pour in plenty of cold water and bring to the boil. Skim off all the foam that forms on the surface. When the foam stops rising, add the remaining ingredients plus 5 ice cubes. Bring back to the boil, then lower the heat so the liquid is simmering. Leave to cook for 2 hours. Skim occasionally to remove any fat and impurities that rise to the surface.

Pass the stock through a colander set in a bowl, and then through a fine sieve. When the stock has cooled completely, refrigerate or freeze it.

Bruno's notes

● The ice cubes will encourage fat and impurities to rise to the surface so they can be skimmed off.

● If you are freezing the stock, use 500 ml or 1 pint bags as these will be the most convenient for further use.

Poultry Jus

Jus de Volaille

1 kg/2¼ lb turkey and chicken
   wings

a carcass from a roast chicken
   (optional)

200 g/7 oz carrots

200 g/7 oz celery

250 g/9 oz onions

vegetable oil

1 tbsp tomato paste

1 bouquet garni (page 209)

3 garlic cloves, crushed with the
   side of a knife

300 ml/10 fl oz white wine

Makes

1 litre/

1⅔ pints/

1 quart

With a cleaver or heavy knife, chop the turkey and chicken wings and chicken carcass into small pieces. Cut the carrots, celery and onions into 2 cm/¾ inch dice.

Heat a film of vegetable oil in a large heavy pot, add the pieces of wings and bones and cook until nicely browned, stirring frequently. Add the diced vegetables and cook, stirring, to give them a golden colour. Stir in the tomato paste, then add the bouquet garni and garlic.

Deglaze with the wine, stirring well, and boil until reduced to 4 tablespoons. Pour in enough cold water to come about 5 cm/2 inches above the ingredients, stir to mix and bring to the boil. Leave to simmer for 2 hours, skimming as necessary.

Strain through a colander set in a bowl, then pass through a fine sieve into a clean pan. Bring to the boil and boil until reduced to about 1 litre/1⅔ pints/1 quart.

● This *jus* goes well with roast or grilled chicken, or it can be used for *pommes fondante* (page 138). It also makes a delicious glaze for macaroni or other pasta: reduce it until it is syrupy, then flavour with chopped herbs, garlic or whatever you like and toss with the freshly cooked pasta.

Bruno's notes

- Frozen in small quantities, it is an excellent standby to make a base for sauces.
- Don't add any seasoning: this is the base for other sauces and salt and pepper will be added to them.

White Veal Stock

Fond Blanc de Veau

Makes about 1.5 litres/ 2½ pints/ 1½ quarts

1 kg/2¼ lb veal trimmings and bones
300 g/10 oz onions, chopped
1 bunch of celery, chopped

1 bouquet garni (page 209)
10 black peppercorns, coarsely crushed with the side of a knife
2 pinches of salt

Put the veal trimmings and bones in a large pot and add enough cold water to come 5 cm/2 inches above the bones. Bring to the boil. When simmering begins, foam will form on the surface; skim this off. When no more foam is rising, add the remaining ingredients and leave to simmer for 3 hours. Replenish the water from time to time to keep the ingredients covered.

Strain the stock through a colander set in a bowl, then pass through a fine sieve.

Bruno's notes

- This stock can be used in a risotto. Or, with the addition of some cream and a sprig of fresh rosemary and then boiled to reduce, it will become a delicate sauce for pasta or boiled meat. It is also excellent for braising celery hearts.
- The small amount of salt added is not for seasoning but helps to draw out the impurities from the veal trimmings and bones.

Veal Jus

Jus de Veau

150 ml/5 fl oz vegetable oil

1 kg/2$\frac{1}{4}$ lb veal trimmings, preferably fatty ones from the breast

100 ml/3$\frac{1}{2}$ fl oz tarragon vinegar

500 g/1 lb 2 oz/2$\frac{1}{2}$ cups canned tomatoes (drained weight)

400 g/14 oz onions

200 g/7 oz carrots

100 g/3$\frac{1}{2}$ oz celery

100 g/3$\frac{1}{2}$ oz mushrooms

4 litres/7 pints/4 quarts cold water

5 garlic cloves, halved

a bunch of fresh thyme

a few parsley stems (about 10)

$\frac{1}{4}$ bay leaf

Makes

2 litres/

3 $\frac{1}{2}$ pints/

2 quarts

Heat 100 ml/3$\frac{1}{2}$ fl oz of the oil in a large roasting pan until very hot. Add the veal trimmings and stir well with a wooden spoon to mix with the oil. Turn the heat down and cook until the meat has exuded all of its juices. These will then caramelize and become sticky and golden. Deglaze the pan with the vinegar and the tomatoes, stirring well to mix with the caramelized juices. Remove from the heat and put aside.

Cut the vegetables into large dice. Heat the remaining oil in a large heavy saucepan and add the vegetables. Cook on a moderate heat until they are lightly browned, stirring occasionally. Pour in the water and add the veal mixture, the garlic cloves and herbs. Bring to the boil, then leave to simmer for 2$\frac{1}{2}$ hours, skimming from time to time.

Strain the stock through a colander set in a bowl and then through a fine sieve.

● You can store the *jus* in containers or bags in your freezer. Or reduce it to 500 ml/16 fl oz to obtain a *glace de veau* (veal essence) and chill in the refrigerator until set. Then cut into cubes, wrap separately and freeze.

Bruno's note

Fish Stock

Fumet de Poisson

Makes

1 litre/

1⅔ pints/

1 quart

500 g/1 lb 2 oz fish bones and heads
    from brill, sole or whiting
100 g/3½ oz onions
75 g/2½ oz leeks
75 g/2½ oz celery
75 g/2½ oz bulb fennel

200 ml/7 fl oz dry white wine
6 coriander seeds
4 black peppercorns
a branch of fresh thyme
1 litre/1⅔ pints/1 quart cold water

Rinse the fish bones and heads under cold running water for 5 minutes to clean them thoroughly.

Finely chop all the vegetables and put them in a large saucepan. Add the wine, spices and thyme. Bring to the boil and boil for 5 minutes, then add the fish bones and heads. Cover with the water and bring back to the boil, skimming the surface to remove all the scum and impurities. Leave to simmer for about 15 minutes.

Strain the stock through a colander set in a bowl and then through a fine sieve. Use as required.

Bruno's notes

- Do not cook the stock longer than 20 minutes because after that it will become bitter.
- You can store this stock in the refrigerator in a covered container for 3 or 4 days, and you can freeze it as well.

Salsa Verde

Sauce Verte

1 green sweet pepper, halved and
seeded

150 ml/5 fl oz olive oil

1 tbsp water

$\frac{1}{2}$ tbsp capers

1 tbsp chopped fresh flat-leaf
parsley

$\frac{1}{2}$ tbsp chopped fresh basil

2 tsp chopped fresh mint

2 tsp Dijon mustard

1 garlic clove, chopped

juice of $\frac{1}{2}$ lemon

4 servings

Put the green pepper in a small saucepan with 1 tablespoon olive oil and the water. Cover and cook over a very low heat for 10 minutes. Remove from the heat. When the pepper is cool enough to handle, peel off the skin.

Combine the peeled pepper flesh and juices from the saucepan with the remaining ingredients in a blender or food processor. Blend until smooth.

Cooked Tomato Sauce

Sauce Tomate Cuite

**Makes
about
500 ml/
16 fl oz/2 cups**

1.2 kg/2 lb 10 oz ripe plum-type or
    other well-flavoured tomatoes
olive oil
200 g/7 oz onions, chopped
5 garlic cloves, crushed with the
    side of a knife

1 sprig of fresh rosemary
1 strip of orange zest
salt and freshly ground pepper
2 tbsp extra virgin olive oil

Cut the tomatoes across in half and squeeze to remove the seeds. Chop the tomatoes roughly.

Heat a film of olive oil in a heavy saucepan and cook the onions until they are soft, stirring occasionally. Add the tomatoes, garlic, rosemary and orange zest and mix well. Cover with the lid and leave to cook gently for 30 minutes.

Discard the rosemary sprig and strip of orange zest. Turn the mixture into a food processor and process until smooth. Pass through a fine sieve. Season with salt and pepper. Reheat for serving, then add the extra virgin oil.

Uncooked Tomato Sauce

Sauce Tomate Crue

350 g/12 oz fresh ripe plum–type
  tomatoes
$\frac{1}{2}$ tbsp red wine vinegar
2 tbsp olive oil

1 slice of white bread, crusts
  removed
1 garlic clove, finely chopped
salt and freshly ground pepper
sugar (optional)

4 servings

Cut the tomatoes across in half and squeeze the halves to remove the seeds. Put the tomato halves in a blender or food processor and add the vinegar, olive oil, bread and garlic. Process until smooth. Season with salt and pepper, then press through a fine sieve.

Taste the sauce. If the tomatoes are too acidic, you may want to add a pinch or two of sugar.

● The quality of this sauce is based on the delicate fresh flavour, so prepare it in small quantities only when you need it.   **Bruno's note**

Rouille

This spicy sauce is usually served with fish soup, but you might also like to try it with poached or grilled fish. Other ideas are to serve it with crudités or grilled aubergine (eggplant) as a starter.

4 servings

120 g/4 oz peeled boiled potatoes

yolk from 1 hard-boiled egg

$\frac{1}{2}$ tbsp Dijon mustard

2 raw egg yolks

150 ml/5 fl oz olive oil

6 saffron strands soaked in the juice

of $\frac{1}{2}$ lemon for 5 minutes

1 tsp salt

$\frac{1}{2}$ tsp harissa or more to taste

Combine the potatoes, hard-boiled egg yolk, mustard and raw egg yolks in a food processor. Process to a smooth purée. Gradually add the olive oil through the feed tube, with the machine running. When all the oil has been incorporated, add the saffron and lemon juice mixture, the salt and harissa. Taste the sauce and add more harissa if you like it very hot!

Your guests may wonder what this rich green oil is, but on first taste they'll swoon with pleasure.

Herb Oil

Huile aux Herbes

1 handful of fresh basil leaves and sprigs pulled from thick stalks, or more to taste	500 ml/16 fl oz olive oil	**Makes**
	1 garlic clove, crushed with the side of a knife	**500 ml/**
2 handfuls of fresh flat-leaf parsley leaves, or more to taste	salt	**16 fl oz/**
		2 cups

Bring a small pan of salted water to the boil. Plunge the basil into the water and blanch for 5 seconds, then remove and refresh in cold water; drain. Blanch the parsley for 10 seconds, then refresh and drain. Squeeze the herbs to remove excess water. Chop them coarsely.

Put the herbs into a blender or food processor and add the oil, garlic and salt. Blend until the oil becomes green and the herbs seem to have disappeared. Strain the oil through a fine sieve, pressing well. Keep it in a covered container in the refrigerator.

Just before using, hold the container under running hot water for a few seconds to warm the oil to room temperature.

● The easiest way to blanch the herbs is to put them in a fine-mesh wire basket. That way you can dip them into the boiling water, lift out and then dip into iced water to refresh. Without a basket you'll have to chase them around the pan of water with a slotted spoon.

Bruno's note

Mayonnaise

Makes	salt and pepper	1 tsp Dijon mustard
350 ml/	$\frac{1}{2}$ tbsp white wine vinegar	150 ml/5 fl oz each vegetable oil
12 fl oz/1$\frac{1}{2}$ cups	2 egg yolks	and olive oil, mixed together

Dissolve 2 pinches of salt and a pinch of pepper in the vinegar. Set aside.

In a large mixing bowl, whisk together the egg yolks and mustard. Gradually add the mixed oils, whisking energetically. When the mixture has thickened and all the oil has been added and absorbed, whisk in the vinegar. Taste the mayonnaise and correct the seasoning if necessary.

Bruno's notes

- You can keep the mayonnaise in a covered container in the refrigerator, but don't store for longer than 3 days as the egg yolks are raw.

- For a simple blue cheese dressing, combine 3 tbsp mayonnaise, 50 g/1$\frac{2}{3}$ oz Roquefort cheese and 3 tbsp water in a blender or food processor. Process until smooth.

Lemon Dressing

Vinaigrette au Citron

3 pinches of sugar

salt and pepper

100 ml/$3\frac{1}{2}$ fl oz water

100 ml/$3\frac{1}{2}$ fl oz lemon juice

300 ml/10 fl oz olive oil

100 ml/$3\frac{1}{2}$ fl oz vegetable oil

**Makes
600 ml/
1 pint/2 $\frac{1}{2}$
cups**

Dissolve the sugar and 3 pinches of salt in the water and lemon juice. Add the oils and 2 pinches of pepper and mix well. Pour into a bottle and seal.

Shake the dressing well before using.

Olive Oil Dressing

Vinaigrette à l'Huile d'Olive

100 ml/$3\frac{1}{2}$ fl oz white wine vinegar

$3\frac{1}{2}$ tbsp water

1 sprig of fresh rosemary

1 strip of orange zest

salt and pepper

300 ml/10 fl oz olive oil

2 garlic cloves, crushed

**Makes
450 ml/
15 fl oz/1 $\frac{3}{4}$
cups**

Combine the vinegar, water, rosemary and orange zest in a saucepan. Add 4 pinches of salt and 2 pinches of pepper. Bring to the boil, then remove from the heat, cover and leave to infuse until completely cold.

Strain the vinegar mixture and add the olive oil and garlic. Mix well. Pour into a bottle and seal.

Shake the dressing well before using.

Pommery Mustard Dressing

Vinaigrette à la Moutarde de Meaux

Makes
500 ml/
16 fl oz/2 cups

salt and pepper
100 ml/3½ fl oz tarragon vinegar
100 ml/3½ fl oz water

1 tbsp Moutarde de Meaux or
   other whole grain mustard
200 ml/7 fl oz vegetable oil
100 ml/3½ fl oz walnut oil

Dissolve 5 pinches of salt in the vinegar and water. Add the mustard, oils and 3 pinches of pepper and mix well. Pour into a bottle and seal.

Shake the dressing well before using.

Balsamic Vinegar Dressing

Vinaigrette au Vinaigre Balsamic

500 ml/16 fl oz red wine

$\frac{1}{2}$ bay leaf

100 ml/$3\frac{1}{2}$ fl oz balsamic vinegar

salt and pepper

100 ml/$3\frac{1}{2}$ fl oz olive oil

100 ml/$3\frac{1}{2}$ fl oz hazelnut oil

100 ml/$3\frac{1}{2}$ fl oz vegetable oil

Makes

900 ml/

1$\frac{1}{2}$ pints/

3$\frac{3}{4}$ cups

Put the wine in a saucepan with the bay leaf and bring to the boil. Boil until reduced to a syrupy consistency. Remove from the heat and leave to cool completely.

Discard the bay leaf, then pour the red wine reduction into a bowl. Add the balsamic vinegar, 5 pinches of salt and 2 pinches of pepper and whisk to mix. Add the oils and mix well. Pour the dressing into a bottle and seal.

Shake the dressing well before using.

- This is perfect for dressing the vegetables left from a *pot-au-feu* (page 106).
- Put a few drops of this dressing on a slice of country bread and top with a slice of air dried ham (San Daniel, Bayonne or Parma). This is simple but delicious.

Bruno's notes

French Dressing

Vinaigrette

Makes
450 ml/
15 fl oz/1$\frac{3}{4}$
cups

salt and pepper

100 ml/3$\frac{1}{2}$ fl oz red wine vinegar

3$\frac{1}{2}$ tbsp water

2 tsp Dijon mustard

2 garlic cloves, crushed with the
side of a knife

300 ml/10 fl oz vegetable oil

Dissolve 3 pinches of salt in the vinegar and water. Add the remaining ingredients, with 2 pinches of pepper, and mix well. Pour into a bottle and seal.

Shake the dressing well before using.

Bouquets Garnis

BASIC BOUQUET GARNI

1 sprig of fresh thyme

$\frac{1}{2}$ bay leaf

3 parsley stalks

1 leek leaf

Hold the thyme, bay leaf and parsley stalks together and wrap the leek leaf around them. Tie tightly with string.

BOUQUET GARNI FOR GAME SAUCES

1 sprig of fresh thyme

1 bay leaf

3 parsley stalks

2 fresh sage leaves

1 strip of dried orange peel

1 leek leaf

Hold the thyme, bay leaf, parsley stalks, sage leaves and orange peel together and wrap the leek leaf around them. Tie tightly with string.

Curry Mix

Poudre de Curry

For centuries, spices have played an important role in gastronomy. Once they were valued as highly as gold (saffron still is) and were a source of great wealth. Today, reasonably priced and widely available, spices are the joy of all good cooks. When used with understanding, they give a lively, enjoyable and subtle accent to dishes.

One evening at Bistrot Bruno I served a dish of fish in a curry sauce to Josceline Dimbleby and her son Henry. They felt strongly that the dish would have been better if I had prepared my own curry mix rather than using bought curry powder. The next afternoon I was in my kitchen working like an alchemist, trying different mixtures until I achieved the right blend.

---

3 tbsp coriander seeds

8 green cardamom pods, crushed
   and bits of pod removed

1 black cardamom pod, crushed
   and bits of pod removed

1 tsp cumin seeds

1 tsp fenugreek seeds

2 whole cloves

2 tbsp white mustard seeds

1 tsp white peppercorns

1 dried bay leaf

$\frac{1}{4}$ tsp dried hot pepper flakes

$\frac{1}{4}$ tsp dried garlic or garlic powder

2 tbsp turmeric

Put the coriander seeds, cardamom seeds, cumin seeds, fenugreek seeds, cloves, mustard seeds and peppercorns in a small frying pan and heat gently for 5 minutes, stirring constantly, until the spices smell very aromatic. Remove from the heat and add the remaining ingredients.

Work the mixture to a powder in a spice mill, coffee grinder or mortar and pestle. Store in a tightly closed jar.

Bruno's notes

- Store spices whole and grind them in small quantities before use.

- If you like your curry mix to be very hot, add more dried pepper flakes or some cayenne pepper.

- The only difficult part of this recipe is grinding the spices finely.

FIGS CARPACCIO WITH RED WINE GRANITÉ, *PAGE 176*

APPLE TART, *PAGE 178*

Grapes in Gin

Raisin au Gin

These are excellent with any game dish, or serve them after the coffee when you are eating with good friends.

---

200 g/7 oz/1 cup sugar

200 ml/7 fl oz water

1 kg/2¼ lb ripe but firm seedless
  green grapes

25 juniper berries

400 ml/14 fl oz gin

1 bay leaf

Combine the sugar and water in a saucepan and bring to the boil, stirring to dissolve the sugar. Remove from the heat and leave to cool.

Take the grapes from the stalks. With a cocktail stick, pierce each grape right through five times. Put them in a sterilized glass jar.

Warm the juniper berries in a small pan until they are aromatic. Leave to cool before adding to the jar.

Pour in the gin and enough of the sugar syrup to cover the grapes. Add the bay leaf. Cover the jar tightly.

Set the jar in a deep saucepan of boiling water (the water should come over the top of the jar) and simmer for 10 minutes. Remove from the pan and leave to cool, then store in a cupboard for at least a month before serving.

Elderberry Liqueur

Liqueur de Sureau

Makes

1.1 litres/

2 pints/5 cups

300 ml/10 fl oz red wine

300 ml/10 fl oz water

250 g/9 oz/1¼ cups sugar

2 strips of orange zest

1 dried bay leaf

2 whole cloves

250 g/9 oz elderberries (weight
  without stalks)

300 ml/10 fl oz brandy

Combine the wine, water, sugar, orange zest, bay leaf and cloves in a saucepan and bring to the boil, stirring to dissolve the sugar. Boil for 2 minutes, then add the elderberries. Boil for 30 seconds longer. Remove from the heat and leave to cool.

Stir in the brandy. Pour into a sterilized bottle or jar, cover and store in a cool, dry place.

Bruno's note

● Gather the elderberries at the end of August and make the liqueur, but do not open the bottle before the end of September.

Chocolate Sauce

Sauce Chocolat

The problem with many recipes for chocolate sauce is that you have to keep them warm in a bain-marie. The sauce here is very convenient because you can keep it for 4 weeks in the refrigerator, and then use it on ice cream or another dessert whenever you fancy.

350 ml/12 fl oz water

110 g/4 oz/$\frac{1}{2}$ cup + 1 tbsp sugar

1$\frac{1}{2}$ tbsp cornflour (cornstarch)

30 g/1 oz/$\frac{1}{3}$ cup unsweetened cocoa powder

1 tbsp instant coffee granules or powder

50 g/1$\frac{3}{4}$ oz dark chocolate

2 strips of orange zest

Kahlua, Grand Marnier or rum to taste

Makes

600 ml/

1 pint/

2$\frac{1}{2}$ cups

Combine 200 ml/7 fl oz of the water and the sugar in a saucepan. Bring to the boil, stirring occasionally to dissolve the sugar.

In a bowl mix the remaining water with the cornflour and cocoa powder.

When the sugar syrup is boiling, stir the cocoa mixture again and then pour it into the pan. Whisk very well. Simmer for 5 minutes.

Add the coffee, chocolate and orange zest and stir until smoothly blended. Remove from the heat, cover and leave to cool completely.

When the sauce is cold, strain it and flavour to taste with your liqueur of choice. Pour the sauce into a jar, cover and store in the refrigerator.

● This sauce will not set in the refrigerator.

● If you want the sauce hot, heat it in the microwave or in a saucepan over low heat, stirring with a wooden spatula.

Bruno's notes

Vanilla Cream

Crème Anglaise

6 egg yolks

75 g/$2\frac{1}{2}$ oz/6 tbsp caster (granulated) sugar

500 ml/16 fl oz creamy milk

$\frac{1}{2}$ vanilla pod (bean) or $\frac{1}{2}$ tbsp vanilla essence (extract)

In a large bowl mix together the egg yolks and sugar with a whisk until you obtain a white, creamy consistency.

Put the milk and vanilla pod in a heavy-based saucepan (if using vanilla essence, add it later). Heat until the milk boils and rises in the pan, then remove from the heat and pour the milk over the egg and sugar mixture, whisking constantly. Return the mixture to the saucepan and cook on a moderate heat, stirring constantly with a wooden spoon, until the cream thickens and will coat the back of the spoon. Don't let the cream boil.

Strain quickly through a fine sieve into a cold bowl. If using vanilla essence, add it now. When the cream is cold, cover and put it into the refrigerator.

Bruno's notes

- This cream is the base of or the accompaniment to many desserts, and it can be flavoured with different liqueurs, orange zest, chocolate and so on.

- It is important that the milk be boiling before it is added to the egg yolks so that the heat of the milk will start to cook the yolks immediately, and help to kill any harmful micro-organisms that might be present in the eggs. After the egg yolks have been added, the cream must not be boiled or it will curdle.

RECIPES FROM FRENCH BISTROTS

L'Ambassade d'Auvergne

22 Rue Gremier St. Lazare, 75003 Paris   Tel: 00 331 42 72 31 22   Chef: Mr Hun

L'Ambassade d'Auvergne is the most rural of cosmopolitan restaurants. Françoise Moulier, the *patronne*, is dedicated to the food of one of the most beautiful and wild regions in France, the Auvergne. It is a region where man has long enjoyed the bounty from superb natural resources. With generosity and simplicity, these are the ingredients for a wonderful *cuisine du terroire*.

Cabbage and Roquefort Soup

Soupe de Choux et Roquefort

4 servings

50 g/scant 2 oz/3½ tbsp butter

100 g/3½ oz onion, chopped

100 g/3½ oz leek, chopped

80 g/scant 3 oz celery, chopped

100 g/3½ oz good air-dried ham, diced

1.25 litres/2 pints/5 cups water

100 g/3½ oz carrots, cut into sticks

100 g/3½ oz turnips, cut into sticks

100 g/3½ oz potatoes, peeled and cut into small cubes

120 g/4 oz green cabbage, shredded

1 bouquet garni

salt and pepper

50 g/1¾ oz dried butter beans, soaked and cooked

120 g/4 oz Roquefort, cut into small cubes

toasted small croûtons

Melt the butter in a large saucepan. Add the onion, leek, celery and ham and cook until the vegetables are very soft. Pour in the water and bring to the boil. Add the carrot and turnip sticks, potato cubes, cabbage and bouquet garni and season with salt and pepper. Cook for 45 minutes.

Add the butter beans to the soup. Discard the bouquet garni.

Put some cubes of Roquefort in the bottom of each soup bowl. Ladle in the soup and sprinkle croûtons and freshly ground black pepper on top. Serve immediately.

Salad of Pig's Trotters with a Fourme d'Ambert Dressing

Salade de Pied de Porc à la Fourme d'Ambert

4 pig's trotters

1 tbsp coarse sea salt

300 g/10 oz carrots, cut into big
   chunks

200 g/7 oz onions, quartered

200 g/7 oz celery, cut into big
   chunks

1 bouquet garni

2 tbsp red wine vinegar

10 spring onions (scallions), white
   and pale green

3 hard-boiled eggs

3 different kinds of salad leaves
   such as oak leaf lettuce and curly
   endive (frisé)

chopped fresh chives

FOR THE DRESSING

100 g/$3\frac{1}{2}$ oz Fourme d'Ambert
   cheese, any rind removed

100 g/$3\frac{1}{2}$ oz walnut pieces

1 tbsp coarse grain mustard

$1\frac{1}{2}$ tbsp red wine vinegar

salt and freshly ground black
   pepper

6 tbsp walnut oil

4 servings

Put the pig's trotters in a pot of water and add $1\frac{1}{2}$ tsp sea salt. Bring to the boil, then drain in a colander. Rinse well under cold running water. Put the trotters back in the pan and cover with fresh salted water . When the water is boiling, add the carrots, onions, celery, bouquet garni and vinegar. Leave to simmer for 3 hours.

When the trotters are cooked, remove the pan from the heat and leave the trotters to cool in the cooking liquid. When they are cool enough to handle, bone out the trotters with a small knife and wrap them in cling film (plastic wrap). Keep in the refrigerator until you are ready to proceed with the salad.

Chop the spring onions, and sieve the hard-boiled eggs.

To make the dressing, put the cheese and walnuts in a bowl and mash and crush with a fork. Add the mustard and vinegar and season with salt and pepper. Slowly mix in the walnut oil.

Combine the salad leaves, diced meat from the pig's trotters, spring onions, eggs and chives in a salad bowl. Pour over the dressing and toss well together. Serve.

Bruno's notes

- The preparation of the pig's trotters can be done the day before or even up to 48 hours in advance.

- Fourme d'Ambert is an uncooked, unpressed cheese that is ripened for 2 months. It is firm and blue-veined, with a fruity flavour.

Mourtayrol

This is a classic dish from the Auvergne and Rouergue areas of France. It is a kind of soup made from beef, chicken, ham, vegetables and saffron, usually served ladled over slices of country bread. Like all country dishes that use a combination of different meats, the Mourtayrol is a treat for celebrations.

100 g/3½ oz/½ cup dried butter beans

300 g/10 oz beef marrowbone

500 g/1 lb 2 oz carrots, coarsely chopped

3 large onions

3 cloves

1 bouquet garni

black peppercorns

coarse sea salt

1 boiling fowl (stewing chicken), weighing about 1.8 kg/4 lb

800 g/1¾ lb beef (short) ribs

800 g/1¾ lb silverside of beef (beef round)

1.2 kg/2 lb 10 oz oxtail, in pieces

500 g/1 lb 2 oz celery, coarsely chopped

2 g saffron

fresh thyme

2 bay leaves

parsley

100 g/3½ oz air-dried ham or good smoked streaky bacon, diced

vegetable oil

80 g/scant 3 oz/½ cup long-grain rice

1 kg/2¼ lb Savoy cabbage

600 g/1¼ lb leeks

800 g/1¾ lb potatoes

600 g/1¼ lb turnips

10 servings

Soak the butter beans in cold water for 12 hours. Soak the marrowbone for 6 hours, then drain and reserve.

Drain the butter beans. Put them in a pan with fresh water to cover and add 200 g/7 oz of the carrots, 1 onion stuck with a clove, the bouquet garni and a few peppercorns. Bring to the boil, then leave to simmer until the beans are tender. When the beans are cooked, drain them and discard the flavourings. Add salt to taste and set aside.

While the beans are cooking, put the boiling fowl, beef ribs, silverside and oxtail in a very large pot. Cover with water and bring to the boil. Drain and return the meats to the pot. Cover with fresh water and bring to the boil. Spike one of the remaining onions with the remaining cloves and add to the pot with the rest of the carrots, the celery, saffron, thyme, bay leaves, parsley, some salt and a few peppercorns. If necessary, add more water: the level should be about 5 cm/2 inches above the ingredients. Bring back to the boil, then cover and leave to simmer. After 2 hours, remove the boiling fowl and reserve; after another 30 minutes remove the beef ribs and oxtail and reserve; and after a final 30 minutes remove the silverside and reserve. When all the meats have finished cooking, set them aside in a warm place and strain the bouillon.

Preheat the oven to 180°C/350°F/Gas 4.

Finely chop the remaining onion. In a small flameproof casserole cook the onion with the ham in a film of oil until soft. Stir in the rice and add twice its volume of bouillon. Transfer to the oven and cook for 20 minutes.

While the rice is cooking, put the cabbage in a pan of cold water and bring to the boil. Boil for 5 minutes, then drain and rinse under cold running water. Cut out the core from the cabbage and separate the leaves.

Put 2 (heaped) tablespoons of rice on a pair of cabbage leaves and roll up into a neat ball, tucking in the sides. Wrap the ball in a piece of muslin or cheesecloth and twist tightly to press it compactly. Tie with string. Continue making a further nine stuffed cabbage balls in this way, arranging them in a roasting pan as they are made. Half cover the balls with bouillon. Braise in a 160°C/325°F/Gas 3 oven for 1 hour.

Cook the leeks, potatoes and turnips. Poach the marrowbone in a little bouillon for 3 minutes; drain. Reheat all the meats and the butter beans in a little bouillon.

Cut the meats into serving pieces. Arrange some or all on a large platter, with the marrowbone, stuffed cabbage balls, vegetables and butter beans, and moisten everything with a little hot bouillon before serving.

Bruno's note
● I find a mixture of finely crushed black pepper and Maldon sea salt most appropriate with this dish.

Auberge de Noves

Departemental 28, 13550 Noves   Tel: 00 33 90 94 19 21   Chef: Robert Lalleman

After working in some of the best kitchens in Europe, Robert Lalleman returned home to take over the running of his family's restaurant. With the help of his father, Robert has slowly changed, improved and perfected the menu at this beautiful *bastide* *provençale*, nestling on the side of a hill. In summer you are invited to eat under the trees on the terrace. There you can savour Robert's cooking while enjoying the fragrance from the garden and the breath-taking views.

'Real' Chicken Roasted with Garlic and Cumin

Un 'Vrai' Poulet de Campagne Roti à l'Ail et au Cumin

1 free-range chicken weighing about 1.6 kg/3½ lb	200 ml/7 fl oz olive oil	**4 servings**
salt and pepper	500 g/1 lb 2 oz carrots	
2 heads of garlic, separated into cloves, peeled	500 g/1 lb 2 oz new potatoes	
a few fresh thyme sprigs	1 tbsp ground cumin	
a few fresh rosemary sprigs	100 ml/3½ fl oz red wine vinegar	
	500 ml/16 fl oz chicken stock	
	2 tomatoes, quartered	

Preheat the oven to 200°C/400°F/Gas 6.

Season the inside of the chicken with salt, pepper and 1 garlic clove. Put in the herb sprigs. Truss the bird. Heat the olive oil in a flameproof casserole in the oven. Put the chicken in the casserole and return to the oven. Roast until browned on all sides, turning so the bird colours evenly.

Meanwhile, cut the carrots and potatoes into 5 mm/¼ inch thick rounds.

Turn the chicken breast up. Arrange the carrots, potatoes and remaining garlic cloves around the chicken. Season the vegetables with salt and pepper, then sprinkle everything evenly with cumin. Continue roasting the chicken for 45 minutes, basting the bird with the juices in the casserole and gently stirring the vegetables every 10 minutes. At the end of the cooking, the vegetables should be soft and golden brown.

Remove the chicken and vegetables to a warmed platter. Set aside to rest for 15 minutes. Meanwhile, set the casserole over a high heat on top of the stove and deglaze with the vinegar. Reduce until all the vinegar has evaporated, then add the stock and tomatoes. Stir well. Reduce again until you have a sauce-like consistency. Pass through a fine sieve and check the seasoning. Keep warm.

If necessary, reheat the chicken and vegetables in a hot oven for 5 minutes before serving. Carve the chicken in front of your guests.

Creamed Peas with Morels

Velouté de Petits Pois aux Morilles

500 g/1 lb 2 oz shelled fresh peas

250 ml/8 fl oz double (heavy)
cream or crème fraîche

250 ml/8 fl oz chicken stock

salt and pepper

300 g/10 oz fresh morels or soaked
dried morels

50 g/scant 2 oz /3$\frac{1}{2}$ tbsp butter

1 shallot, chopped

250 ml/8 fl oz meat juice or *jus de
veau* (page 197)

a few croûtons to serve

4 servings

Cook the peas in boiling salted water until they are tender (test a few: they should melt in your mouth). Drain and refresh in iced water.

Put the cream and stock in a saucepan and bring to the boil. Mix with three-quarters of the peas. Liquidize in a blender or food processor, then pass through a fine sieve. Add the remaining peas. Season with salt and pepper. Set aside.

Remove the feet from the morels, then cut each one in half lengthways. Rinse thoroughly and drain well.

Melt the butter in a sauté pan over a high heat. When the butter starts to change colour, throw in the morels. Season and add the shallot. Cook until the morels have wilted and given up their liquid. Continue cooking until this liquid has completely evaporated, then add the meat juice. Leave to cook for 5 minutes.

Meanwhile, reheat the creamed peas.

Divide the peas among the plates. Add the morels with a little of their juice and a few croûtons and serve.

Goat's Cheese and Chestnut Tart

Tarte au Banon, Brisure de Châtaignes

5 servings

a *pâte brisée* pastry case of 20 cm/
   8 inch diameter, baked blind

5 *banons affinées* (small round goat's
   cheeses wrapped in chestnut
   leaves)

100 ml/3½ fl oz single (light) cream

1 egg

2 egg yolks

butter

200 g/7 oz peeled and skinned
   chestnuts, crumbled

1 garlic clove, finely chopped

1 bay leaf

200 ml/7 fl oz chicken stock

salad of crisp leaves in a strong
   dressing, to serve

Preheat the oven to 180°C/350°F/Gas 4.

Unwrap the cheeses and remove their skins. Mix the cheese with the cream, whole egg and yolks until well blended. Pour into the pastry case. Bake for 20 minutes or until set.

Meanwhile, heat a little butter in a pan and add the chestnuts, garlic and bay leaf. Cook, stirring, to colour the chestnuts. Pour in the stock and leave to simmer over a low heat until the chestnuts are tender. Drain well.

Spread the chestnuts over the top of the cheese filling. Return to the oven to warm the whole tart.

Serve with a crisp salad tossed with a strongly flavoured dressing.

Restaurant Clos
Les Passementiers (bistrot)

3 Rue G. Tessier, 42000 St Etienne   Tel: 00 33 77 41 87 99   Chef: Pierre Gagnaire

In the Sixties, St Etienne was known as the home of Manufrance, a large company manufacturing many different goods, including shotguns and bicycles. In the Seventies, it was 'The Greens' football team that brought fame and pride to St Etienne. In the Eighties, a chef attracted attention to this city. His reputation grew rapidly and his restaurant became known as one of the best places to eat in France.

Today, in the Nineties, Pierre Gagnaire is still here, in his new elegant futurist restaurant. Pierre Gagnaire loves St Etienne and, with his incomparable style, he is the city's best ambassador.

And for the experience of a lifetime, Pierre Gagnaire's restaurant is at 7 Rue Richelandière, 42000 St Etienne.

Veal in Tuna Sauce

Vitello Tonnato

6 servings

250 ml/8 fl oz white wine

2 onions, each spiked with a whole clove

3 carrots, cut into 2.5 cm/1 inch dice

2 celery stalks, cut into 2.5 cm/ 1 inch dice

1 bouquet garni of fresh thyme, parsley, basil and bay leaf

salt and pepper

1 boneless rump or round of veal weighing about 900 g/2 lb

1 small can of tuna in brine or water, drained and flaked

100 g/$3\frac{1}{2}$ oz /1 cup pine nuts

1 tbsp chopped parsley

100 ml/$3\frac{1}{2}$ fl oz olive oil

juice of 1 lemon

300 g/10 oz mixed salad leaves (*mesclun*)

a little dressing

Bring the wine to the boil in a large pan. Add the the onions, carrots, celery and bouquet garni and enough water to make a bouillon that will cover the veal when it is added. Salt lightly. Leave to simmer for 40 minutes.

Put the veal in the bouillon. Bring back to a simmer, skimming all the foam that rises to the surface. Cook over a low heat for 50 minutes.

Remove the veal and wrap it in a dampened clean cloth; set aside. Strain the bouillon through a fine sieve into a clean pan and boil until reduced to 250 ml/8 fl oz. Leave to cool.

Combine the reduced bouillon, tuna, pine nuts and parsley in a food processor and blend together until smooth. Gradually add the oil through the feed tube with the motor running. Mix in the lemon juice and season with salt and pepper.

Slice the veal (if you chill it in the freezer for 30 minutes first, it will be easier to cut very thin slices).

Toss the salad leaves with a little dressing.

To serve, put the salad leaves in the centre of each plate and arrange the slices of veal around. Cover the meat with the tuna sauce.

Farmhouse Chicken with Parmesan, Candied Grapefruit

Poulet de Ferme au Parmesan, Pamplemousse Confit

---

1 free-range chicken weighing
  1.6 kg/3½ lb, cut into 8 pieces
salt and pepper
½ lime
flour
4 thin slices of San Daniele or
  Parma ham, halved
200 g/7 oz onions, finely chopped
500 ml/16 fl oz dry white wine
  (preferably Italian)

olive oil
300 g/10 oz well aged Parmesan, in
  fine shavings
butter

FOR THE CANDIED GRAPEFRUIT
3 pink grapefruits
sugar
100 ml/3½ fl oz lemon juice
250 ml/8 fl oz water

4 servings

First make the candied grapefruit. Peel the grapefruits, taking all the white pith with the coloured skin. Cut the peel into dice. Separate the grapefruit segments, discarding the membranes and any seeds; set the segments aside.

Put the diced peel in a pan of cold water, bring to the boil and simmer for 2 minutes. Drain, and repeat the blanching twice more. Weigh the blanched peel and mix with half its weight of sugar. Put in a pan and add the lemon juice and water. Cook over a low heat for about 1 hour, stirring occasionally.

Add the grapefruit segments and cook for a further 20 minutes. Leave to cool, then chill in the refrigerator for 24 hours.

Preheat the oven to 190°C/375°F/Gas 5.

Season the chicken pieces and rub them with the lime half. Dredge lightly with flour. Heat a nonstick pan and colour the chicken pieces on all sides; this will take about 10 minutes. Wrap each piece of chicken in a piece of ham and set aside.

Heat a film of olive oil in a sauté pan or wide flameproof casserole and cook the onions until soft and golden. Put the pieces of chicken in the pan. Pour in the wine and heat it to boiling, then set it alight. When the flames have died down, scatter the Parmesan shavings over the chicken pieces and dot with a few pieces of butter.

Cover the pan and transfer it to the oven. Cook for 40 minutes.

Serve in the pan. Accompany with the cold candied grapefruit and toasted slices of country bread.

Potato Gratin with Blueberries

Gratin de Pommes de Terre aux Myrtilles

4 servings	1 kg/2¼ lb medium size new potatoes	250 ml/8 fl oz milk
	soft butter	500 ml/16 fl oz crème fraîche
	100 g/3½ oz/⅔ cup blueberries	2 egg yolks
		salt and pepper

Preheat the oven to 180°C/350°F/Gas 4.

Slice the potatoes very finely and rinse them in a basin of cold water. Drain.

Generously butter a large gratin dish or other shallow baking dish. Layer the potato slices in the dish, scattering the blueberries between the layers. Mix together the milk, cream and egg yolks and season lightly with salt and pepper. Pour over the potatoes.

Bake for 45 minutes or until the potatoes are tender.

M. Gagnaire's note

● The quality of this gratin depends on the thinness of the layered potatoes, so be sure you use a very large dish.

Restaurant Alain Chapel

National 83, 01390 Mionnay   Tel: 00 33 78 91 82 02   Chef: Philippe Jousse

When Philippe Jousse was chosen to replace the great Alain Chapel he faced a challenge: who could possibly take over the kitchen of a man said to be the best chef of this century, a man who in his kitchen had taught some of the best chefs of today?

When I met Philippe Jousse I understood why he had been given this task. He is calm, honest and down to earth, and has all the knowledge and feeling learned from working alongside the master. A real craftsman.

Oxtail Terrine in Vinaigrette

Terrine de Queues de Boeuf en Vinaigrette

2 oxtails, cut into pieces	coarse sea salt	**10 servings**
3 carrots		
1 onion spiked with a clove	FOR SERVING	
1 turnip	2 tbsp chopped shallots	
$\frac{1}{4}$ celeriac (celery root)	1 tomato, seeded and diced	
1 bouquet garni	2 tbsp chopped parsley	
1 tsp black peppercorns	vinaigrette made with walnut oil	

The day before, put the pieces of oxtail in a pot and cover with cold water. Bring to the boil, skimming the foam from the surface. Add the vegetables, bouquet garni, peppercorns and some salt, then cover and leave to simmer for 2–2$\frac{1}{2}$ hours. To check if the meat is cooked, remove a piece to a plate. You should be able to pull the meat easily from the bones. Remove from the heat and leave the oxtail to cool in the bouillon.

Drain the warm pieces of oxtail, reserving the bouillon. Take all the meat from the bones, discarding any fat and gristle. Put the meat in a colander and set a plate with a weight on top. Set aside in the refrigerator.

Pour the bouillon into a pan and reduce it slowly, skimming the top from time to time, until 350 ml/12 fl oz remains. Set aside.

When the meat is set and firm, cut it into 2 cm/¾ inch pieces and mix with the tepid bouillon. Pour into a terrine and leave to set overnight in the refrigerator.

On the day of serving, unmould from the terrine and cut into slices that are not too thick. Arrange them on a serving dish. Sprinkle shallots, tomato and parsley on top and cover with vinaigrette. Leave to marinate for 15–20 minutes before serving.

Le Truffia

This dish originated in central France, around Berry. You can serve it with roast meat or on its own with a salad tossed in a walnut oil dressing.

800 g/1¾ lb potatoes

salt and pepper

3 shallots, chopped

chopped fresh flat-leaf parsley

400 g/14 oz *pâte brisée* (rich shortcrust pastry)

100 g/3½ oz smoked streaky bacon (thick bacon slices), cut across into thin *lardons*

1 egg yolk mixed with 3½ tbsp milk

300 ml/10 fl oz crème fraîche

6 servings

Preheat the oven to 200°C/400°F/Gas 6.

Cut the potatoes into slices about 2 mm/scant ⅛ inch thick. Put into the top of a steamer. Season with salt and pepper and mix in the shallots and parsley. Cover and steam for about 10 minutes or until tender but still firm (al dente).

Meanwhile, roll out about two-thirds of the pastry dough to 2 mm/scant ⅛ inch thickness and use to line a tart mould about 23 cm/9 inches in diameter. Prick the bottom with a fork.

Mix the bacon with the steamed potatoes and leave to cool.

Spread the potato and bacon mixture in the pastry case. Fold in the sides over the filling and brush the pastry with the egg yolk mixture. Roll out the remaining pastry dough and cut to a disc that will fit inside the mould. Lay this over the filling and brush with the egg yolk mixture. Cut a hole in the centre of the pastry lid. Bake for about 30 minutes. Cover the top with foil if it is becoming brown too quickly.

Remove from the oven. With the help of a knife, carefully remove the pastry lid and set it aside. Pour the crème fraîche over the filling and mix in gently. Season with salt and pepper. Replace the pastry lid.

Leave the *truffia* to rest for 10–15 minutes before serving – the potatoes will then have time to absorb the cream.

Roast Fresh Figs with Port on Shortbread, Apricot Compote

Figues Fraîches Roties au Porto sur un Sablé, Une Compote d'Abricots

4 servings

200 g/7 oz *pâte sablée* (rich sweet pastry)

8 ripe figs

100 g/3½ oz /7 tbsp soft unsalted butter

50 g/scant 2 oz/3½ tbsp sugar

100 ml/3½ fl oz red Port

FOR THE APRICOT COMPOTE

8 ripe apricots

sugar

First make the apricot compote. Weigh the apricots; you will need one-quarter their weight of sugar. Cut the apricots in half and remove the stones. Crack the stones with a hammer and take out the kernels in the centre (these have an almond flavour). Put the kernels in a saucepan with the apricot halves and sugar. Cook over a low heat, stirring, until the mixture has the consistency of a marmalade. Set aside.

Preheat the oven to 200°C/400°F/Gas 6.

Roll out the pastry dough to 2 mm/scant ⅛ inch thickness and cut out four discs, each 6 cm/2½ inches in diameter. Place on a baking sheet and bake for about 8 minutes. Cool on a wire rack. Turn the oven down to 180°C/350°F/Gas 4.

Make six incisions in each fig, from the top to the base, then brush each fig with soft butter and coat with sugar. Arrange in a buttered gratin dish. Bake for 10–15 minutes. The figs with give up juice.

Add the Port to the dish and stir to mix with the juices. Spoon this liquid over the figs. Return to the oven and bake for a further 3–4 minutes.

To serve, put a shortbread disc on each plate and spread with a spoonful of apricot compote. Top with a fig and spoon over the cooking juices.

La Ferme du Lyonnais

4 Petite Rue Pijay, 69001 Lyon   Tel: 00 33 78 28 37 26   Chef: Bruno Didier Laurent

In my profession you come across a lot of young people whose ideas and feelings for cooking are governed mainly by early success and finances. But once in a while you find a completely dedicated person. 'Petit Bruno', which is the nickname we used to give him, is one of these special chefs. Now in Lyon, in this lovely little bistrot a few hundred yards from the Opéra, he is producing some exciting cooking. I am sure he will make a name for himself.

Risotto with Red Wine and Gizzard Confit

Risotto au Vin Rouge et Gésiers Confits

olive oil

60 g/2 oz onion, finely chopped

1 small sprig of fresh rosemary

200 g/7 oz /1 cup risotto rice
   (arborio)

500 ml/16 fl oz red wine

200 ml/7 fl oz chicken stock

12–15 pieces of poultry gizzard
   confit

1 garlic clove, finely chopped

40 g/scant $1\frac{1}{2}$ oz /$2\frac{2}{2}$ tbsp butter

salt and pepper

4 servings

Heat a film of oil in a frying pan and add the onion and rosemary. Cook over a low heat until softened, stirring occasionally. Add the rice and stir until it is shiny and coated with oil.

Add a little of the wine and mix well. Cook over a moderately low heat, stirring, until all the wine has been absorbed, then add a little more. Continue adding the wine and then the stock a little at a time, mixing often.

About 5 minutes before the risotto has finished cooking, put the gizzard confit in a frying pan, without any fat, and fry just until the pieces of gizzard are hot. Stir in the garlic, then remove from the heat and keep warm.

Increase the heat under the risotto. It should have a creamy consistency, with the rice firm but tender, so add a little more wine if necessary. Add the butter and stir until it has melted. Season with salt and pepper.

Spoon the risotto into bowls and put the gizzards on top. Drizzle the garlicky fat from the confit around the edge and serve.

Bruno's note

● The gizzard is a digestive muscle in poultry. The only way to cook it is to 'confit' it as it has a very hard, compact texture. Look for gizzard confit in jars in speciality shops. If you can't find it, you can substitute duck leg confit.

Mussel Soup with Lemon Grass

Soupe de Moule à la Citronelle

1 kg/2¼ lb fresh mussels

200 g/7 oz celeriac (celery root)

1 lemon, halved

50 g/1¾ oz shallots, sliced

1 tsp thinly sliced fresh ginger

1 stalk of lemon grass, cut into
   small pieces

a bunch of fresh parsley and
   coriander (cilantro)

150 ml/5 fl oz white wine

350 ml/12 fl oz fish stock (page 198)

500 ml/16 fl oz double (heavy)
   cream

salt and pepper

6 servings

Prepare the mussels, scrubbing and rinsing them thoroughly under running water. Discard any that are gaping open.

Cut the peeled celeriac into thin slices, cutting them as long as possible. Sprinkle with lemon juice to prevent any discoloration.

Put the shallots, ginger, lemon grass, parsley and coriander (reserving a little of the latter), wine and stock in a large pot and bring to the boil. Add the mussels, cover and cook until all the shells open. Drain the mussels in a colander set in a bowl and put them aside.

Strain the cooking liquid through a fine sieve into a clean pan. Bring back to the boil. Add the cream and leave to cook gently, stirring occasionally.

Meanwhile, remove most of the mussels from the shells (keep a few in shell for the garnish). Cook the celeriac in boiling salted water until just tender; drain. Add the mussels and celeriac to the soup.

Add the reserved coriander, finely cut, and a few drops of lemon juice. Season to taste with salt and pepper, then serve.

Pumpkin Tart with Walnuts and Almonds

Tarte de Potiron aux Noix et Amandes

4 servings

200 g/7 oz peeled pumpkin (weight without seeds and fibres), cut into cubes

2 tbsp water

50 g/1¾ oz/½ cup walnuts, chopped

50 g/1¾ oz/½ cup flaked (sliced) almonds, lightly toasted

100 g/3½ oz/packed ½ cup light soft brown sugar

grated zest of ⅓ orange

1 tbsp Armagnac

350 g/12 oz puff pastry

1 egg yolk beaten with 2 tsp water

Put the pumpkin in a heavy pan with the water. Cover and cook over a low heat until the pumpkin is very soft and you can mash it with a spoon. Turn it into a blender or food processor and blend until smooth. Return the purée to the pan and cook gently, stirring, to evaporate any excess liquid. Leave the purée to cool.

Preheat the oven to 180°C/350°F/Gas 4.

Mix the pumpkin purée with the walnuts, almonds, sugar, orange zest and Armagnac.

Roll out the puff pastry dough very thinly – 2 mm/less than ⅛ in maximum – and use to line a 20 cm/8 inch tart mould. Keep all the trimmings.

Put the pumpkin mixture in the pastry case, spreading it smooth. Cut the pastry trimmings into strips to make a lattice top. Glaze the pastry with the egg yolk wash. Bake for 20 minutes.

Serve with an orange liqueur or an orange wine.

INDEX

Gagnaire, Pierre, 225–8
game and poultry, 79–103
game sauces, bouquet garnis for, 209
garbure Béarnaise, 112–13
gardener's snails, 34–5
garlic, 9
   aïoli provençale, 58–9
   bouillon santé, 22
gin, grapes in, 211
ginger: caramelized chicken thighs with garlic
   and ginger, 83
   pheasant 'crépinette' with gingered pear, 96–7
   tripe stewed with ginger, onions and chilli,
   127–8
gizzard confit, risotto with red wine and, 233–4
goat's cheese: goat's cheese and chestnut tart, 224
   hot goat's cheese on grilled vegetables with
   figs, 35–6
   Monday's marrow, 130–1
granité, red wine, 176
grapefruit: farmhouse chicken with Parmesan,
   candied grapefuit, 227–8
grapes in gin, 211
gratin Dauphinois, 135
'Gribiche' sauce, 26–7

haddock *see* smoked haddock
haggis: poached lamb shoulder stuffed with
   haggis, 116–17
   root vegetable and haggis soup, 21
ham *see* Parma ham
hare, jugged, 87–8
hay and salt crust, whole chicken cooked in,
   79–80
herbs: bouquet garnis, 209
   herb oil, 203
herrings *see* smoked herrings
horseradish mayonnaise, 116–17

ice cream: cherry beer, 173
   floating islands with Pernod, 170–1
   green peppercorn, 172
   jasmin tea and lemon parfait, 177
   rice pudding, 174–5
ingredients, 6
Irish stew, 115

jasmin tea and lemon parfait, 177
john dory: pan-fried john dory with rosemary
   and orange 'gastrique', 70–1
Jousse, Philippe, 229–32
jugged hare, 87–8
juniper: beef birds in juniper sauce, 110–11
   grapes in gin, 211
   sour cabbage, 151

kebabs: mackerel kebab with piccalilli, potato

cake and lettuce, 64–5
kidneys: grilled lamb kidneys with a devilled
   sauce, 121–2

Lalleman, Robert, 221–4
lamb: braised neck with onions, peppers and
   saffron, 118–19
   Irish stew, 115
   Monday's marrow, 130–1
   poached lamb shoulder stuffed with haggis,
   116–17
   see also brains; kidneys; tongue
Laurent, Bruno Didier, 233–6
leeks: buckwheat crêpes filled with leeks,
   mussels, cockles and crab, 74–5
   Irish stew, 115
   leek and potato soup with a dash of olive oil,
   17
   smoked haddock cooked in milk, potato and
   leek broth, 62
   warm leek salad with poached eggs and
   lardons, 38–9
lemon, 10
   jasmin tea and lemon parfait, 177
   lemon dressing, 205
   light lemon and blackcurrant gratin, 166–7
   steamed lemon pudding, 163–4
lemon verbena crème brulée, 169–70
lentils: boiled salted pork knuckles with lentil
   salad, 123
   green lentils flavoured with cardamom, 154
   mussels and lentils in spicy pot, 71–2
lettuce: mackerel kebab with piccalilli, potato
   cake and lettuce, 64–5
   peas French-style, 143
lime pickle: roast leg of rabbit on lime pickle,
   85–6
   whole snappers baked with lime pickle and
   coriander, 52–3
liqueur, elderberry, 212
liver: shallot tarte tatin with sautéed chicken
   livers, 49–50
Lyonnaise potatoes, 136

macaroon, coconut and chocolate, 188–9
mackerel: affordable fish soup, 18–19
   crispy mackerel, chilli and herb sauce, 63
   mackerel kebab with piccalilli, potato cake and
   lettuce, 64–5
   see also smoked mackerel
marrow, Monday's, 130–1
mayonnaise, 10, 204
   aïoli provençale, 58–9
   horseradish, 116–17
meat, 104–28
meringue: floating islands with Pernod, 170–1
   light lemon and blackcurrant gratin, 166–7